THE BLACK BELT OF VIRGINIA

Untold Stories of African American History

JEFFREY BENNETT

Published by The History Press
An imprint of Arcadia Publishing
Charleston, SC
www.historypress.com

First published 2026

Manufactured in the United States

ISBN 9781467158473
Hardcover ISBN 9781540299734

Library of Congress Control Number: 2025946017

Notice: The information in this book is true and complete to the best of our knowledge. It is offered without guarantee on the part of the author or The History Press. The author and The History Press disclaim all liability in connection with the use of this book.

For my mother, Patricia Ruth Adams Bennett,
the original writer of the family.

CONTENTS

PREFACE

While doing research and reading on Virginia's Black history from the 1500s through the early 1900s in order to compile this book, I discovered there's so much rich history about Black people in Virginia that is unknown or rarely shared. I didn't learn in formal school that immediately following emancipation, there were numerous Black politicians. I didn't learn that in college, either. I didn't learn that the president of the Underground Railroad was a white man named Levi Colvin from Guilford County, North Carolina, just south of the border with Virginia. I didn't know previously that women were also enslavers. My view of slavery was simply that of the rapist male slave master and enslaved people working in the fields, singing hymns.

My previous knowledge of Black people in the Americas was that our story started with slavery and emancipation and went through Jim Crow and the civil rights era up to today. I didn't know there were so many other vibrant facts to our history within those lines. I wasn't aware of the significant strides made during Reconstruction in only a few years and other things within slavery, such as enslaved people working in factories and transporting goods in boats on rivers. I was also unfamiliar with Black people owning other Black people, as well as vibrant, free Black communities during slavery.

My goals and hope in compiling this concise history are that I can share what I've learned with you all, the reader, and that we can continue to learn how rich history can be and continue to dismantle stereotypes or the normal things that you think you know but may not know all of it. May God bless you all.

PART I

THE BLACK BELT OF VIRGINIA

THE BLACK BELT

The "Black Belt" in the United States was a term popularized in the 1800s and early 1900s describing areas with high Black populations. Although it is unknown who coined the term, notable activist and educator Booker T. Washington attempted to explain it in his book *Up from Slavery*, stating:

> *I have often been asked to define the term "Black Belt." So far as I can learn, the term was first used to designate a part of the country which was distinguished by the color of the soil. The part of the country possessing thick, dark, and naturally rich soil was, of course, the part of the South where the slaves were most profitable, and consequently they were taken there in the largest numbers. Later, especially since the war, the term seems to be used wholly in a political sense—that is, to designate the counties where the black people outnumber the white.*

It's not a surprise that Virginia is in the Black Belt. Although there were earlier unsuccessful efforts at slavery in South Carolina and Florida, the enslaved people who arrived in 1619 disembarked at Hampton, Virginia. This unfortunately would trigger a continuous movement of slavery and disenfranchisement of Black people in the Americas for over four hundred years. Virginia would continue to serve as a port with dominant importation of enslaved people, in addition to South Carolina and Louisiana. In the commonwealth, primary arrival ports for enslaved people were Richmond,

Left: The author looking out at the water over which the first Angolans traveled to Hampton. *Author photo.*

Below: An 1860 U.S. map of enslaved people populations in the United States. *U.S. Department of Agriculture.*

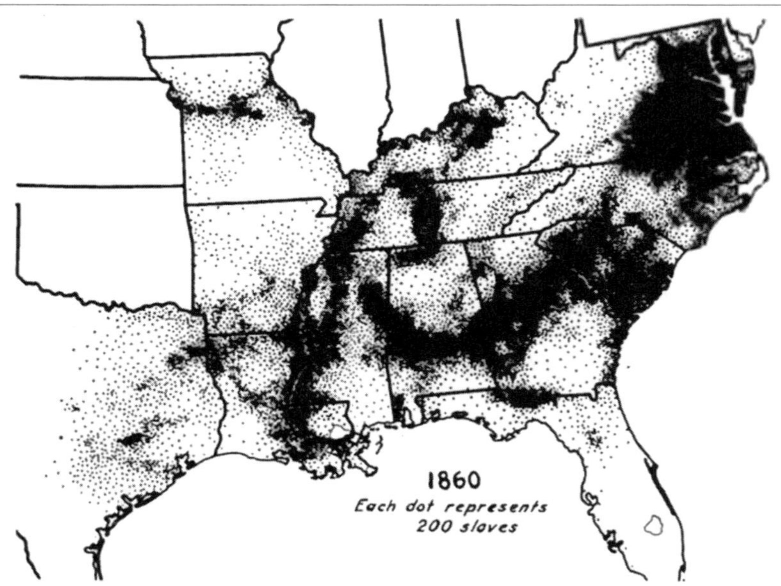

U. S. Department of Agriculture, Bureau of Agricultural Economics. SCALE .8

Number of Slaves in the United States in 1790 and in 1860.

1. These two maps are the first and last of a group of six. Space does not allow all six to be shown here.
2. The use of these two maps in a history lesson would clarify and simplify the slave problem of 1860. This material in tabulated or verbal form would be formidable.
3. Only a section of each map is reproduced here.

Yorktown, Rappahannock, and Fredericksburg. The Shockoe Bottom area of Richmond served as a main trading post for enslaved people. Alexandria also served as a major trading center for enslaved people, especially those being sold from the upper south to lower south regions of Mississippi and Louisiana.

With large numbers of importation of enslaved people from Africa, the Black population began to swell. For example, as noted in the *Washington Post*, "In 1860, more slaves lived in Virginia—490,000—than in any other state in the Union, according to census data."

However, to learn about the significance of Virginia's Black Belt, it is necessary to explore the history of the people before they arrived and explain their histories in West Africa.

West Africa

The thirst for exploration has existed since the creation of man. As early as the 1300s, West Africans had a recorded history in the New World, or what would be known as the Americas. West Africans had notable explorers hundreds of years prior to European exploration. Most notably, Mansa Abubakari II, king of Mali from 1300 to 1311, who had a curiosity about knowledge and foreign lands, left his riches to his brother, Mansa Musa, and landed in Brazil by ship around 1312 to live the rest of his life in the New World. The territories composing his kingdom he left Mansa Musa were significant, amounting to nearly all of West Africa.

Mansa Musa became one of the most celebrated and richest emperors in West African history. His empire stretched across several West African countries, including modern-day Chad, Niger, Nigeria, Mali, Burkina Faso, Guinea, Gambia, Senegal, and Mauritania. He is largely regarded as the wealthiest man in recorded history, with an estimated net worth of U.S. $400 billion.

Roughly a century later and a half later, the Portuguese began to make inroads on the African continent with exploration. They captured a small area at the center of a trade route in northern Africa and then gradually made their way down the West African coast. They were looking for spices and gold, possibly hearing about the riches and gold that Mansa Musa had possessed as king years earlier. In 1441, an exploration team on behalf of King Henry the Navigator kidnapped Africans and took them back to

An artist depiction of Mansa Musa and soldiers. *HistoryNmoor/Wikimedia Commons/CC BY-SA 4.0.*

Portugal to show to the king the potential to enslave people. One of the captives was a noble named Adahu, who was able to negotiate his release back home to Africa in exchange for additional enslaved people. From that experience, the Portuguese continued to return to Africa demanding more captives. This gradual progression unfortunately developed into the transatlantic slave trade.

While expanding south on the western coast of Africa, the Portuguese would eventually work their way down into the area known today as Angola during the 1500s and 1600s. The king in Angola during the time the twenty enslaved people were taken to Virginia in 1619 was Ngola Mbandi, who was on the throne briefly and was succeeded by his sister Njinga a Mbande, who would become known as Queen Nzinga. In a real-life *Game of Thrones*, she fought off Europeans interested in taking captives and brokered several peace treaties throughout her reign, although the Portuguese would be the crux of her existence throughout her three-decade rule.

An 1830s lithograph of Queen Nzinga Mbande. *National Portrait Gallery, London.*

Unfortunately, over time, European traders and greed drove lots of West African kingdoms to fight against one another, with each defeated community becoming captors to the slave trade. People enslaved under the European system were considered property with no rights, or chattel. In the African system, most enslaved people were captives of war, but the terms of their enslavement existed more as a work agreement, comparable to indentured servitude. Additionally, under the African system of slavery, enslaved people had rights, were able to own property, could gain freedom more easily, and could hold high-ranking positions as advisors to kings. It was not the abusive and traumatic unending bondage of the European system.

The ship transporting the twenty Angolans who were stolen was originally headed to Veracruz, Mexico. During a layover in Jamaica, robbers captured the ship, stole the captives, and headed up to Virginia to escape. They landed in the Point Comfort area of what is now Hampton, Virginia, in August 1619.

Before the Angolans landed, they had to endure and survive the Middle Passage across the Atlantic Ocean. They were able to hold onto some traditions and passed them down through generations. Unfortunately, other traditions were lost through the breaking up of families. However, in this new land, they also established new traditions and norms, mostly built out of survival.

In some instances, Africans who were kidnapped had been storing or transporting items in their hair, such as plant seeds. Although it appeared that they didn't have any possessions when they made the voyage, they may have had things such as black-eyed peas, okra, and rice seeds that traveled with them all the way to the Americas. They were able to plant the seeds, nourish, and harvest them in the Americas to maintain some of their culinary traditions from back home.

Traveling the Middle Passage and becoming enslaved in a new land transformed Africans into a new people. Author Ta-Nehisi Coates describes the process of Africans transitioning into African Americans as "the genocide and rebirth of the Middle Passage." Additionally, Robert Hayden describes this process of going through the Middle Passage and becoming new creatures as our "voyage through death / to life upon these shores."

FREE BLACK COMMUNITIES

Despite the trite stereotypes of slavery, there was more to the institution than Black people laboring in the fields and singing hymns. Black people did everything—they piloted cargo on boats, built railroads, worked in factories, and made wine, whiskey, and beer. Additionally, vibrant communities existed for Black people who were not enslaved, known as free people. Although far from being recognized as full citizens, they were able to exercise a reasonable degree of autonomy over their lives. Some were able to earn money and buy their freedom. Others ran away when enslaved and were adopted into free communities. Most who ran away headed north to free Black cities like Philadelphia or farther north to Canada. The Fugitive Slave Act of 1850 changed everything. By empowering enslavers to recapture fugitives even in the so-called free states, it meant that freedom seekers were never truly safe until they crossed into Canada. Harriet Tubman understood this with clarity. "I wouldn't trust Uncle Sam with my people no longer," she said. "I brought them all clear off to Canada."

During the late eighteenth and nineteenth centuries, thousands of enslaved African Americans risked everything to escape northward on the Underground Railroad, seeking freedom in Canada. Many settled in Nova Scotia, New Brunswick, and Ontario, where free Black communities took root despite poverty and discrimination. These settlements were not just refuges of survival; they became centers of cultural innovation.

One such innovation was hockey. Oral traditions and historical accounts trace some of the earliest games of stick-and-ball on ice to Black enclaves near Halifax, Nova Scotia. By 1815, long before hockey was formalized as a Canadian national pastime, residents of the Northwest Arm, including descendants of freedom seekers, were skating on frozen rivers, batting wooden pucks across the ice, and shaping what would become a global sport.

Sometimes, enslaved people may have chosen less popular routes to freedom, whether intentionally or through directional confusion; some escapees headed south and landed in Mexico. Sometimes, it was better to head where you were least expected, even if that meant going through several states that enslaved people.

Mexico abolished slavery in 1829, decades before the United States. Its southern border, lined with ranchlands and river crossings, became a beacon for those willing to risk everything. The journey was perilous. Some fled by night across scrubland and desert, aided by sympathetic Tejanos, Indigenous guides, or free Black allies. Others sought passage by sea, stowing away on ships bound for Jamaica, the Bahamas, or British-controlled islands where slavery had been outlawed.

These escapes formed what historians now call the Southern Underground Railroad, a hidden network of crossings and sea routes that carried men, women, and children away from bondage. U.S. slaveholders raged at Mexico's refusal to return fugitives, and this clash over freedom became one of the sparks behind the Texas Revolution itself. The very existence of Mexico's sanctuary challenged the economic and moral foundations of slavery in the American South. Others opted to stay in the state and were adopted into free Black or Indigenous communities.

The first freeborn Black person in America, William Tucker, was born in the Jamestown area in 1623. His parents, Anthony and Isabella, were part of the original twenty enslaved people who landed in Hampton in 1619.

Of the original twenty Angolans, the following is noted by the *Ebony Pictorial History of Black America*: "Some attained full freedom and some even acquired land or were baptized and obtained the right to vote. Several became affluent and masters of servants of their own. And one is said to have risen to become the master of a white servant."

Additionally, some of the other earlier Africans who arrived after the original twenty did well. One such man, Anthony Johnson, arrived in Virginia from Angola in 1621. Over time, he won his freedom alongside his wife, Mary, and bought land, and they tried to do the best they could as colonized former Angolans.

FREE BLACKS

Under the initial system of indentured service, Black enslaved people and Irish people paying for their voyage to the New World were able to obtain freedom. For Black people, this was short-lived. Anthony and Isabella more than likely gained their freedom, but after the change from indentured servitude to perpetual slavery, millions of enslaved people had no hope of gaining their freedom except through emancipation, running away, or death.

POCAHONTAS ISLAND

Over time, Black people who were able to buy their freedom or were emancipated began to form free Black communities. City hubs like Richmond had prominent free Black communities. These communities had the ability and resources to shield runaways and send them along to free areas such as Philadelphia or Canada. Petersburg, just twenty minutes south of Richmond, also had a prominent free Black community. First Baptist Church of Petersburg, established in 1774, is regarded as the oldest Black Baptist church in the United States and had both free Blacks and enslaved people in its congregation. This interaction could have led to enslaved people strategizing for freedom. It wasn't always an escape plan though, as sometimes other free Blacks purchased enslaved Blacks' freedom, free and clear. By 1860, Petersburg had attained the largest free Black community in the South, with over 3,200 free people of color. One specific free Black community in Petersburg was known as Pocahontas Island (which is actually a peninsula), formed in 1752. Enslaved Africans were first brought there in 1732 to work in John Bolling's tobacco warehouses, and by the early 1800s, it was home to over 300 free Blacks who worked as boatmen, fishermen, and watermen. Among its notable residents was Joseph Jenkins Roberts, who went on to become the first president of Liberia. It is regarded as the oldest African American community in the United States. This community also harbored a stop on the Underground Railroad, located at a house in the community. The neighborhood has endured over time and remains today.

A Pocahontas Island sign during the 2024 election cycle. *Author photo.*

Gum Springs

Another free Black community in Virginia, known as Gum Springs, formed in Fairfax County, just down the road from George Washington's residence at Mount Vernon. West Ford was born as an enslaved person to the Washingtons and eventually served as the caretaker of Mount Vernon in his later years. He was born to an enslaved woman named Venus and a white father. Oral family history from the Fords about their ancestor attests that West Ford was the biological son of President George Washington. Others speculate George's nephew Bushrod Washington was the father. Although unconfirmed, a sketch of West in his early years bears a striking resemblance to the first president. When West turned twenty-one, he was given 160 acres of land by the Washington family and was taught a trade, becoming a skilled woodworker. The Washingtons didn't grant this favor to any other enslaved people. Ford later sold this land and acquired 214 acres in Fairfax County on what he would name Gum Springs in 1833. This became a thriving community for free Blacks and still exists today.

Israel Hill

Free Blacks of Israel Hill historic marker. *Author photo.*

Although Thomas Jefferson had some antislavery sentiments, he emancipated only two people while living. His cousin Richard Randolph, however, was able to emancipate enslaved people whom he reluctantly inherited as an abolitionist through his father's will, freeing over ninety people in 1810 and granting them four hundred acres of land in Prince Edward County. In Melvyn Patrick Ely's book *Israel on the Appomattox*, he states the following about Randolph: "His ex-slaves gave the name Israel Hill to their new home in the rolling terrain of Prince Edward County, as they called themselves 'Israelites.' This was their Promised Land, to which they had been delivered out of bondage."

Additionally, many considered the community "prolific…of many good free negros" of "ability" and "integrity…very much respected and trusted by all classes of citizens."

Black people in the Israel Hill community worked a variety of professions. Some farmed, and others worked as bateauxmen, hauling cargo along the Appomattox River in shallow boats to hub cities like Richmond, Petersburg, and Lynchburg.

Improvised Communities

Black people worldwide have made unthinkable places communities for survival. In Benin, West Africa, fleeing the slave trade, they made a floating community on the lake. In Jamaica and Haiti, runaway enslaved people ran to steep mountain terrain to make maroon communities. In the Americas, some of the earlier Black populations ran away and befriended the Indigenous communities and were adopted. In eastern Virginia, some runaways made communities in the Great Dismal Swamp, where they were hard to reach. It is estimated that thousands of Black and Indigenous people lived there.

Harriet Beecher Stowe's historical novel *Dred: A Tale of the Great Dismal Swamp* recounts the lives of people living in the swampland communities.

For nearly two centuries, the Great Dismal Swamp on the Virginia–North Carolina border was more than a forbidding wilderness—it was a refuge. Stretching across two thousand square miles of quicksand, peat bogs, dense thickets, and alligator-ridden waterways, it offered protection to thousands of enslaved people who risked everything to vanish into its depths. Slave catchers rarely pursued them into such treacherous terrain. Inside, those fugitives, known as maroons, built timber homes, carved out small farming plots, established hidden trade networks, and at times raided nearby plantations. The swamp became both a shield and a stronghold, proof that freedom could be wrestled from even the harshest environments.

In 1856, the illustrator David Hunter Strother ventured into the swamp for *Harper's Magazine*. Guided by two Black men, he froze when he saw a gaunt figure in tattered clothes carrying a gun. The man passed silently, and Strother's companions later whispered his name: Osman. According to historians, Osman was likely born enslaved but had escaped to live among the maroon settlements. He may have been on his way to barter at an outpost, moving between isolation and contact as many swamp dwellers did. His fleeting appearance was a glimpse into a hidden world most outsiders never saw.

Stories like Osman's reveal the Great Dismal Swamp not just as a landscape of danger but as a site of endurance and defiance. For the thousands who made it their home, the swamp was less a place of despair than a testament to human resilience, the creation of an autonomous, secretive society on land meant to keep them trapped. In its bogs and shadows, freedom took root.

Black Mountain (Dan Fields)

Like the maroons of Jamaica and Haiti, some Black people in the central and southwestern mountainous areas of Virginia formed free Black communities during slavery. In rural Wise County, a Black community of about forty-six free people, informally known as Dan Fields, formed atop Black Mountain. Despite what may seem to be challenging circumstances to live in, the community was still able to farm the land and live abundantly. The leader of the community, Dan Richmond, was able to acquire up to 985 acres in Virginia and neighboring Kentucky.

Richmond, previously enslaved to Jonathan Richmond in southwest Virginia, was able to make the Black Mountain community home. In 1879, traveler Charles Johnson recalled a pleasant interaction with Dan Richmond when he requested a place to stay for the night. Richmond responded to him by saying: "Young man, we'se colored folk living hyeh but if you want to stay we'll treat you as best we can," the man answered kindly. "We don't have much but you're welcome to what we have. We don't see many folks up here on the mountain. Up here it's jes' us and the Lawd."

The Richmonds had a family practice of reading a Bible scripture lesson each night before retiring. Dan would read the lesson, and then the family would sing two or three hymns. Johnson recalled:

> *The melodies were sweeter than any I had ever heard before.... The old man (Dan Richmond) followed with an emotional prayer. After another song the service ended. There in a humble mountain home, kneeling at a family altar, was a black family whose souls had been washed in the blood of the Lamb and made as white as snow. I was touched by the goodness of God as I had been touched by Mr. Richmond and his family.*

In later years, coal companies became interested in the parcel of land, and Richmond successfully negotiated a buyout agreement.

BROWN MOUNTAIN CREEK

Another improvised Black community was known as Brown Mountain Creek in Amherst County. Mose Richeson, the mulatto son of plantation owner Jesse Richeson, was able to acquire money working at his father's mill while enslaved and purchase property in Amherst County. Richeson was able to capitalize on his land by renting cabins and land to formerly enslaved people through sharecropping. A smaller community of about eleven families was able to farm and raise livestock. One of the sharecroppers in the community, Taft Hughes, described the sharecropping process: "My dad paid a fourth of the crop. If you owned your team, you only paid a fourth, but if you didn't own your team and the landlord had to furnish a team, you had to give half of what you made." The community was later sold to the U.S. Forest Service in the early 1900s.

FREE BLACK PEOPLE WHO OWNED ENSLAVED PEOPLE

As previously mentioned, slavery existed in the motherland, but not as it existed in the States. Not uncommonly, some free Black people owned enslaved people. Renowned cabinetmaker and free Black person Thomas Day purchased his wife's freedom. She lived in Virginia, while he relocated to North Carolina. He's listed in the census in 1860 as owning two enslaved people with six total people in his house. One of those two enslaved people was more than likely his wife.

Most Black owners of enslaved people, like most white owners of enslaved people, owned a handful of people. As noted, "By 1830, there were 3,775 black (including mixed-race) slaveholders in the South who owned a total of 12,760 slaves, which was a small percentage of a total of over two million slaves then held in the South. 80% of the black slaveholders were located in Louisiana, South Carolina, Virginia and Maryland."

Further, in 1830, the *Journal of Negro History* noted that 948 free Blacks in Virginia owned enslaved people. Of those 948, 348 were women. It was rare to own double-digit numbers of enslaved people, but one free Black man, Benjamin O. Taylor of King George County, owned 71 enslaved people.

Historian James Oakes reasons that Black people owning enslaved people was an act of goodwill, stating, "The evidence is overwhelming that the vast majority of black slaveholders were free men who purchased members of their families or who acted out of benevolence." After 1810, southern states made it increasingly difficult for any slaveholders to free slaves. Often the purchasers of family members were left with no choice but to maintain, on paper, the owner-slave relationship.

EFFORTS AGAINST FREE COMMUNITIES

The American Colonization Society and Liberia

With the growing angst among the white population about free Black communities negatively influencing enslaved people, various strategies were brainstormed to protect the institution of slavery. Most whites thought that free Blacks would negatively influence enslaved people to strive for freedom. Additionally, whites knew free Blacks had more resources to help runaways escape to freedom, such as the case with Ona Judge and various others.

In 1806, the Virginia General Assembly passed legislation that required enslaved people who were emancipated to leave the commonwealth no later than twelve months. Although on paper this seemed like a step in the right direction for white owners of enslaved people, the policy was rarely enforced. Further, insurrections by enslaved people, such as Gabriel's failed insurrection in Richmond and Nat Turner's successful insurrection in Southampton County, gave further incentive for white owners of enslaved people to rid the state of free Blacks, as both events were believed to be abetted by free Blacks providing resources and coordination.

Following Gabriel's attempted insurrection in 1800, Governor Monroe and President Thomas Jefferson corresponded covertly about the possibility of the removal of all free Black people, as it was assumed Gabriel's effort was coordinated by free Blacks. This led to further legislative efforts for free Blacks to leave or be re-enslaved.

Thus, an organization was finally formed with the goal to send Black people back to Africa. This seemed benign on the surface, but the organization wasn't formed to return Black people to their original West African homes; instead, it was organized to send colonized Black people to the colonized West African country of Liberia. As Ta-Nehisi Coates states in his book *The Message*:

> *In 1816, a group of white elites decided that, in the matter of Black people, ethnic cleansing would be preferred to enslavement. The American Colonization Society was formed with the explicit goal of shipping as many Blacks as possible back to their national home—Africa.... Thus Liberia was born—and plagued, for much of its history, by its colonial past.*

Further, when explaining the true intent of the American Colonization Society (ACS), scholar Merton Dillon mentioned the following: "The ACS wanted to expunge blacks from the historical record through emancipation and emigration to Africa."

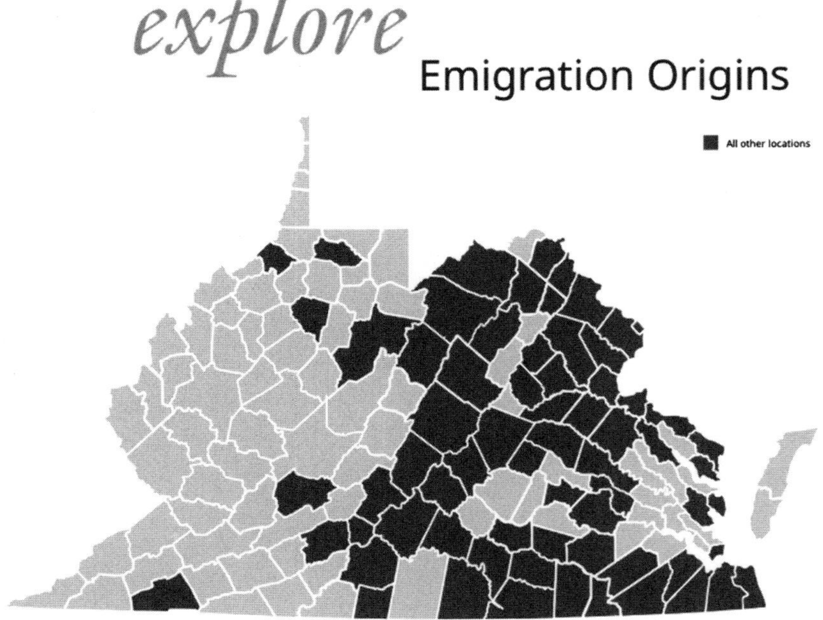

Emigration areas from Virginia to Liberia map. *The Institute for Advanced Technology in the Humanities, University of Virginia.*

Many abolitionists were against African colonization and the ACS. Moreover, many free Blacks shared David Walker's sentiment about the effort to drive them away: "Do they think to drive us from our country and homes, after having enriched it with our blood and tears?"

Ships were filled with Black people departing from Norfolk en route to Liberia. Some benign owners of enslaved people, or people who had a change of heart about the institution of slavery, felt the best thing for them to do was to free their enslaved people and send them to Liberia.

From 1820 to 1866, an estimated 3,700 Black people (mostly free but some enslaved) from over 120 communities throughout Virginia were sent to Liberia by the ACS. Further, as Deborah Lee notes:

> *Black Virginians emigrated, some only because it was a condition for freedom. Given the opportunity to go to Liberia, however, the vast majority of African Americans in Virginia, as elsewhere, refused. They were daunted by the high mortality rate from tropical diseases and, most of all, preferred to stay in the land of more immediate ancestors, in the communities and nation they knew and helped build.*

THE ENSLAVED

It is said that you could walk from Africa to America
on the backs of her stolen children and never would a boot get wet.
—anonymous

Virginia held the most enslaved people in the South by 1860 with over 490,000 people. Although some Black people were able to live free or even make it back to the motherland, according to the *Ebony Pictorial History of Black America*, most enslaved people "arrived in chains and died in chains."

Slavery was so profitable that traders were able to make more money selling enslaved people already in the United States to other areas of the United States than by importing them directly from Africa. As documented by the Library of Virginia, "Between 1790 and 1860, the United States witnessed a great slave migration, with almost 1.1 million enslaved blacks taken out of the upper South destined for the Deep South. Virginia alone exported more than 360,000 enslaved people during this time."

The Exploited

To say that enslaved people were not intelligent because they were not allowed to read would be false. They still had ideas and imagination. They were still cunning, smart, and brilliant. For example, a formerly enslaved person explains how another enslaved person came up with the invention of the railroad, stating the following:

> *My Master tole us dat de n-----s started the railroad, an' dat a n----r lookin' at a boilin' coffee pot on a stove one day got the idea dat he could cause it to run by putting wheels on it. Dis n----r being a blacksmith put his thoughts into action by makin' wheels an' put coffee on it, an' by some kinder means he made it run an' the idea wuz stole from him an' dey built de steam engine.*

Beyond the daily exploitation of laboring in the fields; breeding; working as blacksmiths, cooks, and servants for no pay; and the constant threat of violence, Black people were exploited in other ways. Medical advances were quickened with the unwilling exploitation of enslaved people. In Richmond, enslaved people were forced to rob graves of bodies from Black cemeteries to supply the Medical College of Virginia (Virginia Commonwealth University's predecessor) and other medical schools in the state and East Coast with cadavers. Medical school students would then perform experiments on the stolen bodies. Enslaved people were unfortunately exploited in life and death.

Additional medical advances occurred during the Civil War at the unfortunate expense of enslaved people. When there were not enough vaccines available to combat smallpox, Confederate doctor James Bolton infected enslaved people, predominantly children, to see if he could obtain more lymphs from their bodies needed for the vaccines. In addition to being used like lab rats, enslaved people were treated like livestock. Like every other pro-slave state, when the British ordinance was passed in 1820 against international slave trading, Virginia had to take alternative measures to maintain and increase its labor force. Unfortunately for enslaved people, slave owners and traders would encourage the mass reproduction of people, or breeding, to increase the labor force.

The notorious Lumpkin Jail in Richmond was a holding pen for enslaved people and a breeding farm. When forced to reproduce, enslaved people were required to wear hoods over their heads to conceal their identities. This was done as owners and traders of enslaved people were so desperate and greedy to increase the population of enslaved people that they would often have them reproduce with family members.

An enslaved boy laboring. *Public domain.*

The horrific practice of breeding is described in Encyclopedia Virginia:

> *Enslaved women were commonly referred to in terms that reduced them to their reproductive capacity. Massie recalled hearing enslaved women sold at the local slave auction being referred to as a "fine wench" or a "good breeder." Similarly, some enslaved men with imposing physical builds were used as "stock men" to impregnate a number of women with no regard for family connections. One slave recounted being forced to reproduce with fifteen women and fathered dozens of children.*

The breeding practice was similarly confirmed by formerly enslaved person Maggie Stenhouse: "Durin' slavery there were stockmen. They was weighed and tested. A man would rent the stockman and put him in a room with some young women he wanted to raise children from."

Thomas Blackshear of Orange, Virginia, wrote an article titled "The Selection of Breeding of Negro Slaves." The article describes the practice in intimate details akin to handling livestock. In his manifesto, he mentions the following:

> *Slave breeding is quite profitable as a form of asset reproduction. For example, one common or low-quality breeding wench can produce upwards of 20–25 common stock negro offspring for the market over 20 to 25 years period.... The negro assets produced can be leveraged as collateral for bank loans.*

The Owners

Not only did the distinguished planter class own enslaved people, but other dignitaries such as elected politicians did as well. Historically, over 1,800 politicians nationwide owned enslaved people, including 299 house representatives and 35 senators from Virginia. Inevitably, the way they enacted laws reflected how they lived. A key point in the Constitution reflecting the bias of slavery in politicians of the time was drafting the document to have enslaved people count as three-fifths of a person for the benefit of representation to southern landowners.

In addition to politicians, women also owned enslaved people. What may seem like a horror tale is actually the stark reality of the peculiar institution. In Montego Bay, Jamaica, Annie Palmer owned Rose Hall Plantation, which held over two hundred enslaved people. Palmer wasn't the typical belle like those portrayed in *Gone with the Wind*. She was a menace, known to have killed her three husbands and also forced enslaved people to have sex with her and then eventually killed them.

In Virginia, women who owned enslaved people didn't carry the reputation of Palmer, but they weren't pushovers either. Ruth Hairston became the owner of Berry Hill Plantation in southside Pittsylvania County. However, Berry Hill wasn't the only plantation the family owned. The Hairstons were significant figures during slavery, owning fifty-four plantations in Virginia, North Carolina, and Mississippi, totaling over ten thousand enslaved people.

Her family member Sam Hairston was regarded as the richest man in Virginia and one of the richest men in the South. Ruth became a plantation owner by chance, not by choice. Her husband chose to start a plantation in Mississippi, leaving her to handle Berry Hill.

Another Virginia woman owner of enslaved people, Fredrika Bremer, showed the independence necessary to run a plantation. As mentioned in Stephanie Rodger-Jones's book *They Were Her Property*:

> *Fredrika Bremer was not content with simply visiting slave markets. She also traveled to the slave jails of Virginia, where slave people were held until their owners were ready to sell them and into a slave pen in the District of Columbia....She went to the slave pen with a precise idea of the kind of slave she wanted to buy, and she knew how much she wanted to pay for him.*

Ruth Hairston and Fredrika Bremer were not anomalies, as noted further in *They Were Her Property*:

> *Individuals in cities and towns throughout the south regularly held auctions, just for women, at which they could bid upon a variety of items such as bedsteads, bureaus, chairs, carpets, and mattresses, as well as a splendid assortment of rich dress goods and trimmings, elegant silk cloaks, wool blankets counterpains, quilts, and housekeeping articles....These auctions were well attended; sometimes crowds of 100 or more women would pack themselves into the auction rooms.*

Female owners of enslaved people didn't simply buy people to work in the house as cooks and maids or in the fields tending to crops and livestock; some female owners took it a step further by operating "negro brothels" with their enslaved people laboring as prostitutes for them.

Men were historically noted as sexual exploiters of enslaved people. As noted in the Encyclopedia Virginia, the commonwealth had the largest number of mixed-race enslaved people of all the southern states, totaling approximately forty-four thousand in 1850.

Further sexual exploitation was also driven by women. Thomas Buckley's analysis illuminated the following details:

> *Divorce in antebellum Virginia, roughly 9 percent of Virginia's divorce petitions from 1786 to 1851 were for interracial adultery, with twenty-*

> *three of those petitions coming from white men who complained about their wives' relationships with Black men. Peter Neilson, traveling in Virginia in the 1820s, recorded that he had learned about a "planter's daughter having fallen in love with one of her father's slaves, had actually seduced him."*

Women engaging with enslaved people was even played out on the big screen in the 1975 movie *Mandingo*, with the plot based on a white woman forcing a Black enslaved man to regularly have sex with her, resulting in an undesired pregnancy.

Emancipators

There were also instances when slave owners granted their enslaved people freedom through their wills. This was the slave owners' last chance to absolve their sins when leaving this life. President George Washington emancipated his 124 enslaved people in his will to be effective upon his wife's death, with the exception of William Lee, his personal servant, who was manumitted immediately upon Washington's death. Unfortunately for the rest of the enslaved people, they were not granted freedom when Washington's wife died.

Mural of enslaved people transporting cargo on a bateaux boat. Artists Kitty Williams and Jack Stone. *Museum and Archives of Rockingham County, Wentworth, NC.*

Thomas Jefferson had a desire to emancipate all enslaved people; however, his actions were not able to match his sentiments, and he emancipated only 5 people in his will.

A friend of James Madison and Thomas Jefferson, Robert Carter III of Northumberland County, emancipated the largest number of enslaved people in Virginia history seventy years prior to the Civil War. In 1791, Carter freed over five hundred enslaved people. Further, to help with their transition to being free people, he helped them lease or buy land, made sure they had skills to make a living, and even bought products they sold.

There were also lesser-known examples of the everyday folks who emancipated their enslaved people. For example, in 1790, a female owner of enslaved people in Pittsylvania County, Anne McDaniel, willed freedom to one of her enslaved women. Her testament states the following:

> *I, Anne McDaniel of P, being conscience* [sic] *that the Doctrine of Christ teacheth us to do unto others as we would they should do to us and having a Negro Woman Slave in my possession named Caroline, I do now set free and Emancipate the said slave and her increase, and do for myself my Heirs etc resign and relinquish all my right and title to the said Slave Caroline and her increase. Signed with my Seal this 11th day of November 1790.*

Another emancipator in Pittsylvania County, John Ward Sr., freed all 136 of his enslaved people in his 1826 last will and testament. Of those 136, 70 decided to relocate to Lawrence County, Ohio, a free state.

Industrial Slavery

The most common theme people conjure with slavery is Black people working in fields and singing hymnals. However, this wasn't always the case. Enslaved people who learned a trade, such as carpentry, masonry, or blacksmithing, were able to hire themselves out or be hired out by their masters to do special projects. In Virginia, some cities, such as Lynchburg and Richmond, had enslaved people working in tobacco factories. From producing tobacco in the fields, transporting the crop on the river via bateaux boats, and processing the crop in factories, Black people in Virginia were the driving force behind the cash crop of slavery.

Lynchburg Museum director Ted Delaney attests to the resourcefulness of enslaved people with the following: "They worked in the industries here, the foundries. They built railroads. They excavated the railroad tunnel. They worked as specialty craftsmen, coopers and blacksmiths and all the trades that needed to happen then. And they were really an absolutely essential part of the local economy." Black people are noted as almost half of Lynchburg's population in census records prior to the Civil War.

Other areas of the state, such as Rockbridge County, relied on enslaved labor to further fuel industry work. For example, an advertisement called for twenty Negro slaves for work in the Rockbridge County Iron Works. It stated that the buyer would "provide clothing, lodging and attention during sickness."

Farming

Great farming and land cultivation skills are largely why the American experiment succeeded. Black people were industrious farmers in West Africa and continued to be industrious farmers in the Americas. They were able to cultivate crops such as corn, potatoes, rice, okra, black-eyed peas, and tobacco and tend to livestock. Most plantation owners pushed their enslaved

Bright leaf tobacco historical marker. *Author photo.*

people to work from before sunup to after sundown or, as the saying went, "from can't see to can't see."

Years before the college basketball rivalries of Tobacco Road, the Piedmont region produced leading numbers of tobacco every year in Virginia and North Carolina. The inventor of bright leaf tobacco, known as "Stephen the Slave," came up with this variation of tobacco by accident just across the southern Virginia border in North Carolina, where he was enslaved. Instead of its normal brown color, the tobacco appeared to be a bright gold color due to Stephen accidentally heating it too long during the curing process. This accident worked out positively, as there was a demand for the new gold-colored crop.

Tobacco was known as one of the cash crops of slavery and was surpassed as the premier export only by another crop in the 1800s: enslaved people. Selling enslaved people from Virginia to New Orleans became more profitable than exporting tobacco worldwide, and Thomas Jefferson was in favor of disbanding the international slave trade because more money was made by breeding and selling enslaved people in the colonies than by importing them directly from West Africa. New Orleans became a Black-dominated city over time because of the constant stream of Black people flowing into the city via the slave trade and Haitian immigrants relocating to French-based Louisiana during the Haitian revolution.

Alcohol

Enslaved people were familiar with alcohol, as some received an allotment of alcohol from their owners around the Christmas and New Year's holidays. This was done strategically to keep their minds off running away. Their owners may have purchased the alcohol from other places, or they may have had the enslaved people produce it themselves onsite. This wouldn't be a first for Black people making alcohol, though.

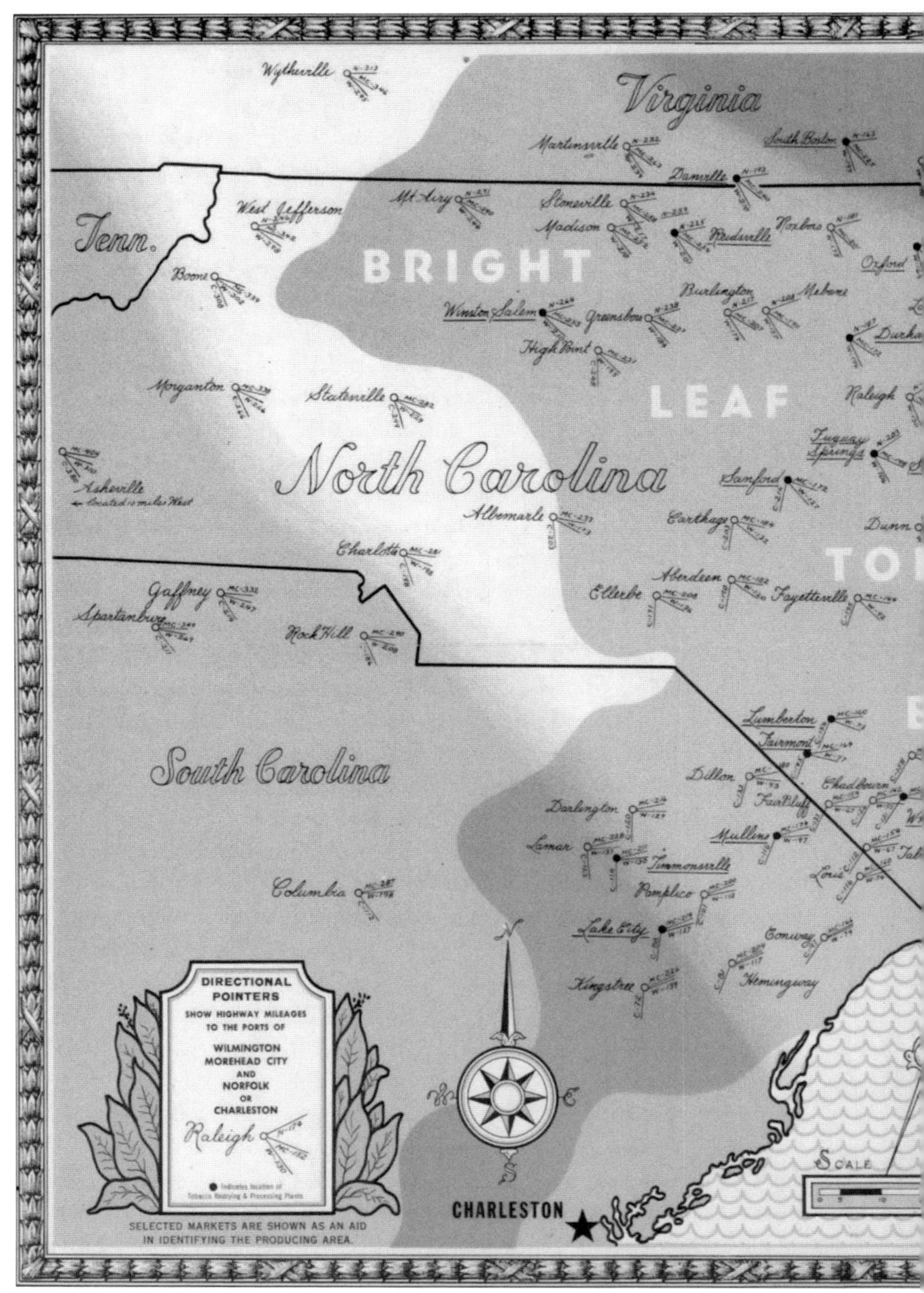
Virginia
Tenn.
North Carolina
South Carolina
BRIGHT
LEAF
DIRECTIONAL POINTERS
SHOW HIGHWAY MILEAGES TO THE PORTS OF
WILMINGTON
MOREHEAD CITY
AND
NORFOLK
OR
CHARLESTON
Raleigh
SELECTED MARKETS ARE SHOWN AS AN AID
IN IDENTIFYING THE PRODUCING AREA.
CHARLESTON
Wytheville
Martinsville
South Boston
Danville
Mt. Airy
Stoneville
Madison
Reidsville
West Jefferson
Boone
Winston Salem
Greensboro
Burlington
Mebane
Oxford
High Point
Durham
Morganton
Statesville
Raleigh
Asheville
Sanford
Albemarle
Carthage
Dunn
Charlotte
Aberdeen
Ellerbe
Fayetteville
Gaffney
Spartanburg
Rock Hill
Lumberton
Fairmont
Dillon
Chadbourn
Darlington
Lamar
Timmonsville
Mullins
Loris
Columbia
Pamplico
Lake City
Conway
Kingstree
Hemingway
SCALE

Bright leaf tobacco map. *Government publication, North Carolina State Ports Authority.*

Winemaking specifically was prominent by 2700 BCE in Egypt, which traded with other African nations on the continent. Additionally, palm wine, from West Africa, had been cultivated and consumed for centuries. The author of a 2020 study on Black wine entrepreneurs, Dr. Monique Bell, mentioned, "Even before America, there were cultures in Africa making and consuming wine. There are anecdotal accounts of black people making wine in the southern US states from native grapes (most likely Muscadine) and fruit trees, but it was just not documented in history books.'

Further, Jefferson School African American Heritage Center curator Leslie Scott-Jones stated, "There would not be 90% of what we enjoy without the ingenuity and intelligence of enslaved people. The knowledge they brought [from Africa] informed what they do here."

Enslaved people were skilled in cultivating crops, such as barley, wheat, hops, and grapes, to make beer, whiskey, and wine. Like Nathan "Uncle Nearest" Green producing alcohol for Jack Daniels, enslaved people also made alcohol for other notable people. Two of the most notable owners of enslaved people who benefited from enslaved labor producing alcohol were Presidents George Washington and Thomas Jefferson.

Thomas Jefferson, a noted wine enthusiast, had 193 acres of property that he specifically used to produce grapes for wine, powered by the labor of enslaved people. Additionally, Jefferson had one of his enslaved people, Peter Hemings, learn the trade of winemaking so that he could produce good wine on-site.

As noted by wine writer Sedale McCall, Jefferson benefited from "efforts from enslaved people like James Hemings, his brother Peter Hemings, and Ursula Granger Hughes, who were critical to the food and wine served at the former president's estate, Monticello."

The skilled trade of making alcohol was also an asset that traders of enslaved people highlighted in advertisements. As noted in a 1745 ad in the *Virginia Gazette*, "To be sold to the highest bidder: A Valuable young Negro woman, very well qualified in all Sorts of Housework, as Washing, Ironing, Sewing, Brewing, Baking." Additionally, as noted in President Andrew Jackson's enslaved person runaway advertisement, he identified enslaved runaway George as "a good distiller."

In addition to laboring for their owners, enslaved people were also able to sell alcohol at markets that they produced from their personal cultivation, as records show George Washington and Thomas and Martha Jefferson also purchased alcohol from enslaved people.

As further mentioned, "Hops was among the most frequently purchased products from the slave community by Martha," wrote author Peter Hatch, former director of gardens and grounds at Monticello. Hops, a plant ingredient used to make beer, were so popular that Virginia was noted as the top-producing southern state in 1860, with 10,015 pounds of hops produced by the labor of enslaved people.

In terms of liquor, enslaved distillers of George Washington at Mount Vernon, Timothy, James, Daniel, Nat, Peter, and Hanson, helped produce eleven thousand gallons of whiskey for Washington in 1799. Whether Washington's, Jefferson's, or Jackson's enslaved people also produced wine for Holy Communion by churches is unconfirmed but highly likely. Black people in southside Virginia who were enslaved and served as clergy when emancipated made jug wine for church communion from locally planted grapevines. It is entirely plausible and likely common that other enslaved people throughout Virginia, including Washington's, Jefferson's, and Jackson's, used wine for church communion.

From the sacrifices of George Jackson; Timothy, James, Daniel, Nat, Peter, and Hanson Washington; Peter Hemings; and all of the anonymous enslaved people lost to history, Black people in America finally broke through to ownership levels during the Great Depression. Born just under thirty years after emancipation in 1894, John Lune Lewis was able to open the first Black-owned winery in the United States, Woodburn Winery, based out of southside Clarksville, Virginia, in 1940.

Escaping Slavery

In southern Virginia, runaways would have likely connected with abolitionist Levi Coffin's network. Known as the president of the Underground Railroad and residing in Guilford County, North Carolina, under an hour south of the Virginia border, before he relocated to Indiana, Coffin had a strong network of antislavery coordinators and resources that could have routed them along the Underground Railroad to Indiana, along to Illinois or Michigan, and then over into Canada.

Like Harriet Tubman, known as the Moses of her people, another Moses was integral to the Underground Railroad and Union army efforts. Moses Dickson was born free in Cincinnati, Ohio, to parents who had migrated from the Petersburg, Virginia area. Trained as a barber, he soon became a minister and a powerful voice for abolition and self-determination within free Black communities. In 1846, at just twenty-two years old, Dickson organized a clandestine Black liberation army, known as the Knights of Liberty. They drilled in secret, established cells across slaveholding states, and by the mid-1850s claimed to have over forty-two thousand members ready to mobilize. Their plan was to launch a coordinated national uprising centered in Atlanta in 1857, with the aim of marching through the South, freeing enslaved people, and fighting slaveholders in open battle. Though the massive revolt the Knights envisioned never materialized, the organization laid the groundwork for coordinated resistance and mutual aid among African Americans across several states.

When the Civil War erupted, Dickson and many of his associates redirected their energy toward the Union cause. He worked to recruit Black men into the Union army, ensuring that African Americans were not only fighting for their own liberation but also reshaping the meaning of freedom in the nation's struggle. His wartime efforts reflected his lifelong conviction that freedom had to be secured through organization, discipline, and collective action.

George Henry

In Alexandria, an enslaved ship captain, George Henry, orchestrated a more elaborate way to gain his freedom than the traditional routes on the Underground Railroad. A noted ship captain in the area, he labored for and gained the trust of his enslavers. He and a five-man crew routinely delivered products such as grain, logs, bark, and timber to the port cities of Baltimore and Annapolis. In South Carolina, Robert Smalls bravely stole and sailed a Confederate ship to Union lines to safety. He further helped the Union navy during the Civil War, and later, he went back to South Carolina to buy the plantation on which he was previously enslaved and became an elected official. In an escape less heralded than Robert Smalls's but equally courageous, George Henry sailed his ship to Baltimore, left it docked, and then took a boat and train to the free city of Philadelphia. He took it upon himself to take control of his life at a time when his life wasn't his own legally. In his own words, Henry mentioned in his memoir the following: "I was determined to let them [white slaveholders] see that though black, I was a man in every sense of the word."

Ona Judge

Ona Judge, once an enslaved person to George and Martha Washington at Mount Vernon, managed to run away to freedom in New Hampshire in 1796. She had been reared on the Washington plantation as the son of a white indentured man and Black enslaved woman, classified as mulatto. She gained favor within the Washington family and worked as one of nine enslaved people who rotated between Mount Vernon and Philadelphia, where the nation's capital was located at the time, to support the Washingtons during the presidency. While in Philadelphia, she was able to lean on the robust free Black community to help her escape. In her own words from an 1845 interview, she mentions, "Whilst they were packing up to go to Virginia, I was packing to go, I didn't know where; for I knew that if I went back to Virginia, I should never get my liberty. I had friends among the colored people of Philadelphia, had my things carried there beforehand, and left Washington's house while they were eating dinner."

Through the network of free Black people, she was able to take a ship from the port of Philadelphia to Portsmouth, New Hampshire.

Two days following her escape, the Washingtons issued an advertisement for her capture stating the following:

> *"Oney Judge" had "absconded" from the president's house and offering a $10 reward for her recapture. Kitt described the young woman's "very black eyes and bushy black hair," noting that she was "of middle stature, slender, and delicately formed." She had "many changes of good clothes, all sorts," Kitt warned and might be trying to pass as a free woman, escaping on a ship leaving the port of Philadelphia.*

Although the Washingtons had considerable reach, influence, and resources to recapture runaway enslaved people, Ona Judge proved savvy and determined, remaining uncaught.

Later in life, she was asked if she had any regrets over fleeing enslavement from the Washingtons. She responded by saying, "No, I am free, and have, I trust been made a child of God by the means."

Harry Washington

Like Ona Judge, Harry Washington began life enslaved at George Washington's Mount Vernon estate. Restless under bondage, he first attempted escape in 1771 but was captured and returned. Yet the Revolutionary War soon offered a new opening. When the British promised freedom to the enslaved who joined their cause, Harry fled again, this time for good, joining Lord Dunmore's Ethiopian Regiment and later serving with the Black Pioneers. After the war, his name appeared in the *Book of Negroes* as one of the thousands of Black Loyalists evacuated to Nova Scotia in 1783. Though free, he found poverty and discrimination waiting, and in 1792, he boarded a ship to Sierra Leone to help build a new colony for liberated Africans.

Even there, Harry's fight for true freedom was unfinished. In Sierra Leone, he became a vocal dissenter against colonial taxation and injustice, taking part in an 1800 rebellion that was crushed by British troops. Exiled to Bullom Shore, he likely died soon after, far from the Virginia fields where his struggle began. Like Ona Judge, who fled Martha Washington's grasp in Philadelphia and lived out her life free in New Hampshire, Harry Washington claimed his liberty through courage and defiance. Their stories—one ending in exile, the other in quiet endurance—stand as testaments to enslaved people's determination to seize freedom from even the most powerful hands in early America.

If Ona Judge and Harry Washington remained enslaved, their teeth may have been used to fill in George Washington's dentures, like others who were enslaved by him. Historical records, including his own financial ledgers, show that Washington purchased teeth from enslaved people. For example, in 1784, he paid several unnamed enslaved individuals for nine teeth, which were then likely used in his dental prosthetics.

BLACK PEOPLE'S RELATIONSHIP WITH INDIGENOUS POPULATIONS

1526

In some instances, Indigenous people enslaved Blacks to go along with the colonizer mentality. However, in most cases, Indigenous people were allies to Black people, often hiding them, providing safe shelter, and allowing them to assimilate into Indigenous communities as runaways.

Prior to full colonization, when the Europeans went on their exploration journeys to the New World, they used African interpreters to translate with Indigenous people as early as 1453. As historian J. Leitch Wright Jr. states, "Both white and Indians relied heavily on Negro interpreters."

In 1526, there was a failed attempt at starting slavery in the New World. Ninety-three years prior to the twenty Angolans landing in Hampton in 1619, Spaniards had kidnapped one hundred Africans and brought them to the South Carolina Lowcountry to start an enslaved community. Roughly two months after their August arrival, the enslaved people led an insurrection against the colonizers who were struggling against illnesses of the New World. The colonizers who remained left, and the Africans were adopted into local Indigenous communities.

York the Explorer

Born enslaved in Caroline County, Virginia, York lived a life of uncommon adventure for an enslaved person. York was enslaved to of William Clark, and they grew up as best friends, were the same age, and often played together. After President Thomas Jefferson acquired the Louisiana Territory from Napoleon, his secretary, Meriwether Lewis, was tasked with exploring the land out to the Pacific Ocean. Lewis reached out to his friend William Clark, and with an exploration crew that included enslaved person York, they headed out west.

While training in St. Louis for their travels, York started learning words of Indigenous origin that would help him along the way. He was also able to help Sacagawea translate. Further, he became so proficient in Indigenous languages that he was assigned the task of trading with Indigenous populations for food. Later in life, he was able to gain his freedom and became a business owner. His interactions with the Indigenous tribes were critical to the success of the journey west.

THE BLACK CHURCH AND ITS SIGNIFICANCE

In addition to her native language, Queen Nzinga spoke fluent Portuguese, which she learned as an understudy when helping her father deal with them. Later, during her reign, she converted to Christianity and was baptized. Anthony and Isabella, two captives on the *White Lion* from Angola who landed in Hampton, were also believed to be Christian before they were captives based on their names. Additionally, their son William was baptized into the church in Virginia.

In the 1500s, the Catholic Church gave approval for the intercontinental slave trade. Centuries later, it gave a formal apology. African leader Kenyatta famously stated, "When the missionaries arrived, the Africans had the land, and the missionaries had the Bible. They taught us how to pray with our eyes closed. When we opened them, they had the land, and we had the Bible." Although some Europeans used religion as a strategy to conquer others, politicizing, weaponizing, and using it as a method to control, religion at its core, untarnished, was something that most Black Virginians valued and participated in.

Church or religious activities during enslavement were offered on a case-by-case basis. If allowed, enslaved people were taught incorrectly on purpose about the apostle Paul calling for slaves to obey their masters. Enslavers didn't want enslaved people learning the entire Bible, especially the Old Testament with Moses leading the Israelites out of Egypt, as their enslaved people could relate, and it may have triggered an insurrection. When worship was not allowed, enslaved people had to worship clandestinely far into the woods, sometimes with bowls over their heads to muffle the sound.

While visiting Danville, a man from the New England area described what he viewed of Black people worshipping in church: "On some southern plantations, planters went as far as to build chapels or 'praise houses' for black worship. Still, most African Americans found their spiritual needs were best met separately and sometimes secretly, holding their own services in brush arbors in secluded areas of forests."

As Henry Louis Gates Jr. explains in his book *The Black Church*:

> *The Black Church offered a reprieve from the racist world, a place for African Americans to come together in community to advance their aspirations and to sing out, pray out, and shout out their frustrations.... The liminal space between slavery and freedom.... The Black Church fueled slave rebellions, nurtured and sustained the Underground Railroad.*

Nat Turner, a preacher and enslaved person in Southampton County, Virginia, drew on his faith when determining to initiate a rebellion against slavery stating, "I had a vision, and I saw white spirits and black spirits engaged in battle, and the sun was darkened." This vision came true, as he witnessed a solar eclipse, a sign that he used to initiate that vision of rebellion.

First Baptist Church of Petersburg historical marker. *Author photo.*

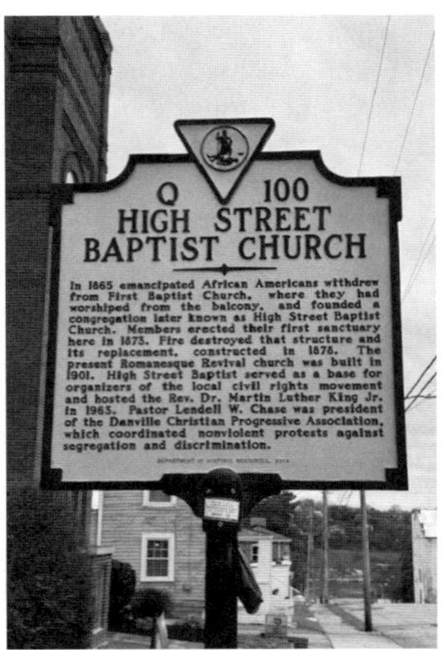

High Street Baptist Church of Danville historical marker. *Author photo.*

Two of the oldest Black churches in the United States are located in Virginia. First Baptist Church of Petersburg traces its beginnings back to 1756. First Baptist Church of Williamsburg was established in 1776, with members originally meeting in fields secretly. Both communities had large free Black populations. Both free and enslaved people worshipped at these churches.

More than anything, the church gave and continues to give Black people hope. The timeless quote by Henry Louis Gates Jr. best describes this by stating, "Preachers helped people live another day, so if things didn't get better for them, they got better for their children and grandchildren."

WAR

Black people are noted as fighting in every war in American history. Needing additional forces during the American Revolutionary War in 1775, Virginia Royal Governor Lord Dunmore was able to recruit Black soldiers with the promise of earning freedom. The Black men who fought were able to wear the phrase "Liberty to Slaves" on their uniforms. In response, General George Washington also recruited Black soldiers for the Continental army. Moreover, the Virginia legislature required all masters to emancipate enslaved people who fought in the war effort.

During the War of 1812, Black people fought in the Battle of Rhode Island and the Siege of Yorktown. As a result of Black people's courageous efforts, Rhode Island ended slavery. Black soldiers took tremendous pride in wearing a uniform and fighting for a cause and their country. As Frederick Douglass stated, "Once let the black man get upon his person the brass letters U.S., let him get an eagle on his button and a musket on his shoulder and bullets in his pocket and there is no power on earth which can deny that he has earned the right to citizenship in the United States."

The Civil War was no different; Black people enlisted to fight. At the start of the Civil War in 1861, there were roughly 4.3 million Black people living in the United States, of whom roughly 400,000 were free and 3.9 million enslaved. This war was more meaningful though, as it would have a direct effect on their future status as enslaved people or newly freed people. Black people risked their lives to escape to Union territory. They could have kept going, maybe to a free state or Canada, but they chose to fight for others—to fight for freedom. Some died in battle. This gave Black men something to believe in and fight for. Additionally, they felt ownership of being a member of society in this country. The thrill of victory that filled Black soldiers' bodies when they saw the white flag rise had to be exhilarating. To be oppressed by white people and then finally have the oppressors surrender made them feel worthy and validated. It made them feel that their sacrifice was justified. In total, over 200,000 Black people served in the U.S. Colored Troops during the Civil War, of whom 5,919 were from Virginia.

Black women were also integral to the success of the war. They served as spies and nurses and sometimes disguised as men on the front lines. Enslaved in Maryland, Harriet Tubman, known to the white folks as the Moses of her people, helped free scores of enslaved Black people and also served as a Union spy. In 2024, the State of Maryland honored Tubman posthumously with a promotion to brigadier general.

One lesser-known but equally significant Union spy, Mary Bowser, also helped the war effort. While Tubman escaped to freedom, Bowser's freedom was purchased by her benevolent and pro-abolitionist former owner, Elizabeth Van Lew. Bowser was free to pursue a new life in the North, but she chose to go back to Richmond in an effort to free her other family members, eventually finding herself as a spy disguised as a servant in Confederate President Jefferson Davis's home. With this fortuitous role, she was able to gather and share information through a network of pro-Union strategists, which helped Union forces prepare for the Confederates' anticipated war strategies.

Mary Bowser, Union spy. *Public domain.*

It was a great climax for the Union army when it was backed up by the Colored Troops in battle, triggering the surrender of the Confederate army. As witnessed by a formerly enslaved person, "The Colored regiment come up behind an' when they saw the Colored regiment they put up the white flag."

The location of the surrender was east of the Israel Hill free Black community by a day's march. The Confederates had recruited a dozen men from the community to support the effort. These men probably supported the Confederates to keep the peace in their community, but after the war, the community was even more relieved to have Black people everywhere live free.

It was further vindication to the Black community when President Abraham Lincoln acknowledged their war contributions, stating, "Without the military help of the black freedmen, the war against the South could not have been won."

AFTER THE WAR

Ownership

Out of enslavement, some communities of people became sharecroppers, while others—such as my relatives—went up to the mountainous areas of Virginia and West Virginia to work in the coal mines. Other folks sought work in factories, relocating to more populated areas, similar to the Great Migration from the Deep South up to cities such as Detroit and Chicago.

One of the many reasons newly emancipated Black communities in Virginia stayed tightknit was because they still had to rely on each other for survival. Unfortunately, after emancipation, some people died off for lack of resources—food and shelter. Virginians were not fortunate enough to receive land from the government like neighboring states to the south. From January 1865 to July 1866, Black people received four hundred acres of land in South Carolina, Georgia, and Florida—land of former plantation owners. However, staunch Confederate supporter and President Andrew Jackson pulled back the land and regifted it to the former plantation owners. Fortunately, resources of free Black people and eventually the Freedmen's Bureau allowed newly emancipated Black folks to be able to build up. And although sharecropping agreements were predatory, the practice also helped Black people survive, albeit it was a meager existence. Over time, Black people began to buy and farm their own land, build businesses, and continue self-sufficient growth.

The Colored Monitor Union Club was a group of free Blacks that formed prior to slavery's end to strategize how to obtain voting rights. They also called for landownership, as stated in their equal suffrage manifesto shortly after the end of the war:

> *The surest guarantee for the independence and ultimate elevation of the colored people will be found in their becoming the owners of the soil on which they live and labor. To this end, let them form Land Associations, in which, by the regular payment of small installments, a fund may be created for the purchase at all land sales, of land on behalf of any investing member, in the name of the Association, the Association holding a mortgage on the land until, by the continued payment of a regular subscription, the sum advanced by the Association and the interest upon it are paid off, when the occupier gets a clear title.*

BLACK-OWNED LAND AFTER EMANCIPATION

Black people's farming, agricultural intelligence, and work ethic carried over after emancipation as many continued, whether in sharecropping or farming on their own land.

A Black family in Northern Neck, Virginia, acquired land for farming. This wasn't uncommon during that time, as a lot of people strove to purchase agricultural property. As noted in Fair Farms Now about the popularity of purchasing land:

> *Black farm land ownership steadily increased in the late 1800s, and hit an all-time-high national average in 1910—when 14% of all farm owner-operators were Black Americans. This was in the decades following the Civil War, in which freed slaves and their descendants accumulated 19 million acres of land. During this Reconstruction period, Black landowners purchased every available and affordable plot of land that they could.*

What is uncommon is that this particular Black family, the Haynies, were able to hold onto their land throughout challenging eras of American history and develop their farm into a commercial business enterprise that is still operating today. Known as Haynie Farms, the business has been fully operational and family-owned for five generations.

In 1867, Robert Haynie, who was formerly enslaved, acquired sixty acres of land in Northumberland County. When talking about the original part of the family land in Heathsville, Ricky Haynie, great-grandson of Robert, mentioned, "This was the first piece of property a black man owned in this whole county." As of 2025, the Haynie family owned several thousand acres, producing soybeans, corn, and wheat primarily.

In addition to farming, Robert Haynie was a preacher and built Macedonia Baptist Church. As noted about Ricky's ancestor Robert, "He believed in two things: the land and his Bible." Those same morals passed forward to his great-grandson Ricky. When talking about the ethics he wants to instill in his family, Ricky mentioned, "Love the lord and the farm. Lisa and I want them to love the Lord, enjoy hard work and appreciate their family."

It is a blessing and a miracle that the Haynie family still farms commercially. It wasn't all smooth sailing and an easy growth trajectory for Haynie Farms over time. They dealt with discrimination from the USDA and local threats from jealous farmers, with their tractors being shot up and over nine hundred of their hogs being burned at one point. They have weathered the storm to be able to contribute admirably back to the continent where their ancestors came from.

Some farmers were modestly successful, but most were just holding on to make ends meet. Calvin Adams Sr., a World War II veteran who fought in the Pacific Theater, worked on a small family farm his family acquired in the early 1900s. After his family moved back to Pittsylvania County from working the coal mines in West Virginia, he and his family farmed the land his grandfather John Breedlove purchased in 1904. John Breedlove started with a 22-acre tract, and in total, he was able to acquire 160 acres of land.

When John Breedlove died in 1941, he owed creditors for the land he had acquired. Selling part of the land would have been sufficient to pay off his debts. Instead, all the land was erroneously sold without the family's consent. The defendant's original attorney, well respected and first African American U.S. trial attorney Martin A. Martin, made a mistake and cut a deal without the authority of his clients. Calvin Adams's family got another attorney and appealed successfully to the Virginia Supreme Court. The local court judgment was proved null and void, and Adams's family was able to retain a fifty-acre tract, with the rest being sold to satisfy John's creditors.

In the court case record, it was argued by the Adamses' attorney that "the real purpose of WH Gray [who took the Adamses' land] was to sell all lands of John Breedlove, a colored man, in a prosperous section of Pittsylvania County."

Calvin Adams Sr. and his wife, Ruth Adams, at their family farm in Pittsylvania County. *Author photo.*

Adams family children on the family farm in Pittsylvania County. *Author photo.*

John Breedlove got a posthumous win. This was also a rare win for Black families in courts during Jim Crow in the southern haven of Virginia.

To pay for the attorney, Calvin Adams sent money he earned in the navy during the war back to his family to fight the case. The family was able to save their farm and continue to make a living, growing kale, corn, turnips, potatoes, and tobacco seasonally. Calvin and most members of the family are buried on the land they farmed and fought to keep.

When discussing Black-owned land in the early 1900s, historian Dr. Cassandra Newby-Alexander stated:

> *In the 1920s, Blacks owned at least 50 to 60% of the land in Virginia. And so there was a systematic effort to take that land, and there were all kinds of laws that were passed that would eventually try to take land. A lot was taken through eminent domain. Look at the Agricultural Adjustment Act. That was to pay farmers not to produce on the land. So what happened to the Black sharecroppers? They were told, "Leave the land. We don't need your labor anymore." Tenant farmers, the same thing.*

Ownership also came in other forms, such as material possessions, companion animals, and businesses. One of the most prized possessions was the family Bible.

As noted by Henry Louis Gates Jr.:

> *In the Reconstruction period, acquiring a Bible was one of the first things people would do in a home because it showed that you were being settled, that you have a place to live, you have a little money, and then also you could study that Bible. You would know scriptures just as well as your pastor did.*

In addition to the Bible, owning a dog also became a status symbol of freedom. According to a California State University report about African Americans relationships with dogs, the following is noted:

> *After Emancipation, for many African Americans, owning a dog came to denote freedom and autonomy. With limited access to homeownership, property, and capital, dogs became the first form of property African Americans could own after slavery. Owning a dog also served as a symbol of self-reliance. In* The Black Man's Burden, *founder of Utica Institute in Mississippi William Henry Holtzclaw wrote: "If we had meat, ten to one it was because 'Old Buck' had caught a 'possum or a hare*

the night before. Many a night the dogs and I hunted all night in order to catch a 'possum for the next day's noon meal." Dogs provided the newly emancipated with an additional means to provide for their families and stood as a source of security in a world rife with discrimination and wanton racial violence. However, this union did not escape the sardonic entertainers of the South.

Dogs became companion animals to enslaved and free people who cared for them during and after the Civil War. A notable story tells of an enslaved person running to freedom who took his dog, Jack, with him during the war. This famous tale became a book and then eventually a movie called *Dog Jack*, inspired by true events. Jed, the main character enslaved in *Dog Jack*, is from Virginia.

Business

Ownership extended beyond land, companion animals, and Bibles. Black people became owners of successful businesses supporting Black communities. After the failure of Freedmen's Bureau's Bank, which was set up by the government to support Black banking but folded due to risky investments, Black people took their destiny in their own hands.

The Savings Bank of the Grand Fountain United Order of True Reformers, founded in 1888 in Richmond by Reverend William Washington Browne, a formerly enslaved man from Georgia, was the first Black-owned bank in the United States. Created to safeguard the financial interests of Black depositors, it provided a secure space free from white oversight and exploitation. Remarkably, the bank thrived during the 1893 economic depression, cementing its legacy as a milestone of Black economic independence and resilience.

In the early 1900s, Maggie Lena Walker emerged as one of the most visionary leaders of Black economic empowerment in America. At a time when segregation and systemic racism shut African Americans out of mainstream financial institutions, she called for the community to build its own bank. "Let us have a bank that will take the nickels and turn them into dollars," she urged, emphasizing the power of collective saving and investment. For Walker, financial independence was more than money—it was dignity, security, and a path to freedom.

Turning her words into action, Walker worked tirelessly to transform her dream into reality. In 1901, she announced her plan for a community-owned bank, and with the help of attorney James Hayes, she pursued a charter from the State of Virginia. On July 28, 1903, the charter was approved by the Virginia Corporation Commission, and the St. Luke Penny Savings Bank officially opened its doors in Richmond. The achievement was monumental: not only was the bank designed to serve Black depositors, but it was also the first bank in the United States to be founded and led by an African American woman.

Walker's vision went far beyond business. By creating a financial institution that reinvested in its own community, she gave Black families access to mortgages, business loans, and savings accounts that were otherwise denied to them. Under her leadership, the bank grew steadily, helping to stabilize the economic life of countless families. In doing so, Maggie Lena Walker demonstrated how collective action could turn small sacrifices into lasting wealth—and how one woman's determination could break barriers of both race and gender in the Jim Crow South. As the daughter of a former enslaved woman and Irishman, Walker's mother was employed by Elizabeth Van Lew, the abolitionist who freed Mary Bowser and helped with Union spy missions during the Civil War.

Reconstruction forced Black people to rely on themselves. They became entrepreneurial and self-reliant. Additionally, they were appreciated as customers more than at establishments that were not Black-owned. From having their destiny controlled previously, this resourcefulness allowed them to control their fate.

Some Black-owned banks post-emancipation in Virginia included First State Bank of Danville, Mechanic and Farmers Bank, St. Luke Penny Savings Bank, and True Reformers Bank. By 1928, there were twenty banks located throughout the commonwealth, with ten based in the eastern part of the state. With the collapse of the Freedmen's Bureau's Bank, Black people chose to build their own.

Education

Church and education became pillars of the Black experience in Virginia and the Americas. These two pillars helped Black people become emotionally mature and astute, building men and women prepared to carve out a place for themselves and communities to survive and prosper.

Black people had a thirst for education, especially since it was prohibited during slavery. They didn't wait for the government to help build them schools; they set about to do it themselves. Most early educational centers were formed out of churches. Black people were creative in using the resources available to them. Being previously denied education, they took their newly legal privilege seriously. As described by the men of the Colored Monitor Club in Norfolk who drafted the Equal Suffrage document, the following is mentioned regarding education:

> *Let him visit the colored schools of this city and neighborhood, in which between two and three thousand pupils are being taught, while, in the evening, in colored schools may be seen, after the labors of the day, hundreds of our adult population from budding manhood to hoary age, toiling, with intensest eagerness, to acquire the invaluable arts of reading and writing, and the rudimentary branches of knowledge.*

COLLEGES

Eventually, Black people were able to build structures devoted primarily to education. Cheyney University in Pennsylvania was the first historically Black college, founded in 1837 by Quakers. The first Black college in Virginia, Virginia Union University, was formed in 1865. Virginia Union has perhaps the most unique beginnings or repurposing of any college in Virginia. What was previously known as the devil's half acre, Lumpkin Jail was located in the Shockoe Bottom area of Richmond and was used as a holding facility and breeding farm for enslaved people being auctioned and sold. Out of this structure, Mary Lumpkin repurposed it to use for Black education. The area where the jail used to be is now known as the African Burial Ground, with an estimated 200,000 people buried there. After the conversion of the area, clergyman and Virginia Union University President Charles Henry Corey stated famously, "The old slave pen is no longer the 'devil's half acre' but 'God's half acre.'"

Following the lead of Virginia Union, Hampton University formed in 1868, with its campus on the former little Scotland plantation. Virginia State University formed in 1882, Virginia University of Lynchburg in 1886, St. Paul's College in 1888, and Norfolk State University in 1935. Further examples of the church and education being the main pillars of

Top: Kingsley Hall under construction, circa 1900. *Public domain.*

Bottom: St. Paul's College sign. *Author photo.*

the Black community can be seen in the formations of Virginia University of Lynchburg, St. Paul's College, and Virginia Union University, as all were established with the backing and support of the church.

Michael Lomax, president and CEO of the United Negro College Fund, once told CNN, "But as church-affiliated institutions, their education provided another element: The education emphasized moral character and community service."

Virginia State University and Virginia Tech are the two land grant universities in Virginia. The Morrill Act of 1862 took land from Indigenous communities and reallocated the land for the formation of land grant universities across the nation.

The Smithsonian Institute refers to philanthropy to Black education with the following: "Philanthropic organizations like the Carnegie Corporation, Julius Rosenwald Fund, and the General Education Board (funded by John D. Rockefeller), however, offered the greatest level of funding and direction to Black colleges at the turn of the twentieth century."

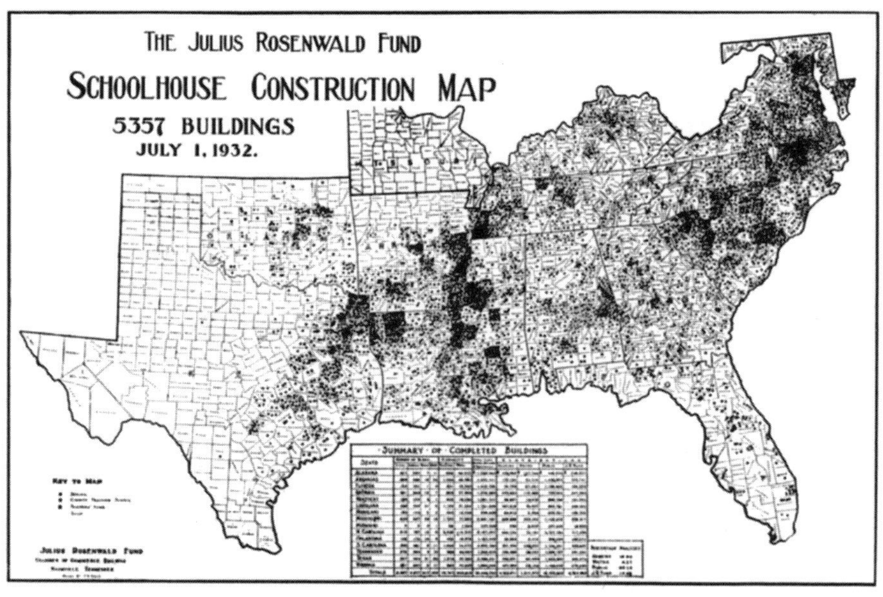

Rosenwald schools map. *Fisk University, John Hope and Aurelia E. Franklin Library Special Collection, Julius Rosenwald Fund Archives.*

Rosenwald Schools

Activist and educator Booker T. Washington, originally from Franklin County, Virginia, helped with the rollout of public schools for Black people in the United States when he was the president of Tuskegee University. He also had influence with Hampton Institute, attending the university and becoming an alumnus. But most notably, he helped with the partnership of the Rosenwald Schools, established by Julius Rosenwald, a philanthropist and businessman who funded the effort through grants from the Rosenwald Foundation. In Virginia, over 350 Rosenwald Schools were funded and built for the advancement of Black education. These schools, in addition to the other Black schools and education happening in the churches, allowed Black people to nurture their intelligence after legally being denied for centuries.

Two other notable schools for Black people were St. Francis de Sales Academy for women and St. Emma Military Academy for men. Like Hampton University, formed on a former plantation, Belmead Plantation in Powhatan was repurposed as a high school for Black students. These were boarding schools that, in addition to core subjects, focused on skilled trades. Both schools operated from the late 1800s to the 1970s.

BLACK POLITICS

Rights

The period from 1865 to 1877 was a significant one for the country, defining Black people's involvement in politics. Free people helped set up key measures to springboard into action once the war was over and the infrastructure for Black people to live independently was in place. Generations removed from West Africa, Black people now identified America as their home and wanted to take every step possible toward gaining citizenship and having equal rights in the country they helped build and defend through military service.

Reconstruction was a time of growth for Black people. Instead of getting on ships back to continental Africa, newly emancipated Blacks decided to make the best of the situation where they were now: America. Black people identified more now as Americans of continental African descent as opposed to continental Africans. This can primarily be attributed to losing some or all of the culture from the motherland. Additionally, America was what they knew. Two primary areas of focus were of importance to Black people during the period of Reconstruction: land and voting rights.

Colored Monitor Union Club

If there was ever a Black version of the Bill of Rights or related document seeking equal footing and demands, the Equal Suffrage document—authored by Black people in Norfolk—would be that equivalent. The Colored Monitor

Union Club was a group of free Black people who formed the organization prior to slavery ending to strategize how to obtain voting rights.

Some key excerpts from their Equal Suffrage document are as follows:

> *We do not come before the people of the United States asking an impossibility; we simply ask that a Christian and enlightened people shall, at once, concede to us the full enjoyment of those privileges of full citizenship, which, not only, are our undoubted right, but are indispensable to that elevation and prosperity of our people, which must be the desire of every patriot.*
>
> *Let the fact that, in the short space of nine months, from what was called the contraband camp, at Hampton, near Fortress Monroe, and from other parts of this State alone, over twenty-five thousand colored men have become soldiers in the army of the United States, attest our devotion to our country. Over 200,000 colored men have taken up arms on behalf of the Union, and at Port Hudson, Olustee, Milliken's Bend, Fort Wagner, and in the death-haunted craters of the Petersburg mine, and on a hundred well fought fields, have fully proved their patriotism and possession of all the manly qualities that adorn the soldier.*
>
> *You have not unreasonably complained of the operation of that clause of the Constitution which has hitherto permitted the slavocracy of the South to wield the political influence which would be represented by a white population equal to three fifths of the whole negro population; but slavery is now abolished, and henceforth the representation will be in proportion to the enumeration of the whole population of the South, including people of color, and it is worth your consideration if it is desirable or politic that the fomenters of this rebellion against the Union, which has been crushed at the expense of so much blood and treasure, should find themselves, after defeat, more powerful than ever, their political influence enhanced by the additional voting power of the other two fifths of the colored population, by which means four Southern votes will balance in the Congressional and Presidential elections at least seven Northern ones.*
>
> *But how can you avoid the charge of inconsistency if you leave one eighth of the population of the whole country without any political rights, while bestowing these rights on every immigrant who comes to these shores, perhaps from a despotism, under which he could never exercise the least political right, and had no means of forming any conception of their proper use?*
>
> *Further, the Congress of the Confederation expressly refused in June, 1778, to permit the insertion of the word "white" in the fourth article of*

Legislature of Virginia, Session 1871 and '72. *C.R. Rees & Co., Richmond, Va., Virginia Legislature Photograph Collection, Visual Studies Collection, Library of Virginia.*

> *Confederation, guaranteeing to the "free inhabitants" of each State, the privileges and immunities of citizens, in all the States. Free people of color were recognized voters in every State but South Carolina, at the time of the formation of the Constitution of the United States, and therefore clearly formed part of the "people" of the United States, who in the language of the preamble to the Constitution "ordained and established" that Constitution.*

The significance of the Black vote can't be overstated enough. By 1867, 80 percent of formerly enslaved Black people had registered to vote. President Ulysses Grant won his election by a thin margin of 300,000 votes. Black people put him in office, with over 500,000 Black people voting for him.

Politics

Black men jumped at the opportunity to serve in public office. They now had a voice and were determined to be heard.

Regarding political service, Wikipedia mentions that more than 1,500 African American officeholders served during the Reconstruction era (1865–1877) and in the years after Reconstruction before white supremacy, disenfranchisement, and the Democratic Party fully reasserted control in southern states.

In Virginia, Black people accounted for 42 percent of the population in 1870, or 512,841 people. Of this population, 85 people held public office during the Reconstruction period. The history of Black people in Virginia has been generalized as starting with slavery, emancipation, Jim Crow, civil rights, and the modern era. But there was a period, albeit a few years, when Black people made significant progress before. Black people had major influence in local politics and helped in drafting the state constitution. For

The 1887–88 members of the Virginia General Assembly. *Bells Mill Historical Research and Restoration Society, Inc., Chesapeake, Virginia.*

a brief period of years after emancipation and before redemption, Black people showed what America could be when the political and social climate was in their favor.

For a short period, Black people were able to show what America could be. This period was an evolution of Black businesses, politics, and pushing for equality. Historian Brent Tarter mentions, "It's no wonder that backward-looking white people were appalled at how fast things were changing—their property was now writing them a constitution."

Unfortunately, the period known as white redemption, starting in 1877, ushered in racial hate incidents and the rolling back of laws that helped Black people until the fight for equality during the civil rights period. But for a period of about fifteen years, Black people were able to show their potential and what they could be in the United States. This amazing group of people defined the Black Belt of Virginia.

PART II

COLLECTED ESSAYS

THE BLACK ANCESTOR OF EUROPE'S KINGS AND THE FIRST TWELVE ENSLAVED AFRICANS

In 1441, two Portuguese captains seized twelve Africans on the coast of what is now Mauritania and carried them across the sea. Among them was Adahu, a Muslim chief who spoke Arabic. Presented in Lisbon as trophies to Prince Henry the Navigator, they were displayed not as individuals with families and histories but as proof of Portugal's daring. Adahu negotiated his own release, promising to provide captives in return. Within a few years, that arrangement had metastasized into something much larger: the organized trafficking of human beings across the Atlantic.

If this episode marked the beginning of the transatlantic slave trade, then its origins carry an irony few Europeans would have recognized. Two centuries earlier, a Black Moorish woman named Madragana had entered the Portuguese royal family as a concubine of King Afonso III. Through her children, she became an ancestor of the very kings and princes who would inaugurate the slave trade. In other words, when Portugal's monarchs turned westward toward Africa, they were condemning people who might have shared blood with their own Black foremother.

Madragana, sometimes recorded as Mor Afonso or Mouroana, was a Muslim noblewoman from the Algarve in southern Portugal. In the thirteenth century, after Afonso III's conquest of the region, she was brought into his household as a concubine. Though medieval chroniclers tended to obscure women like her, enough evidence survives to suggest she was of African descent.

Through her children, Madragana entered the genealogy of Portuguese nobility. Over the following generations, her lineage spread upward and outward into the ruling dynasties of Portugal. By the fifteenth century, the House of Avis, direct descendants of Afonso III, held the throne. These were the monarchs who oversaw Portugal's maritime expansion, celebrated as the Age of Discovery.

Yet discovery for some meant destruction for others. The bloodline of a Black woman helped produce Prince Henry the Navigator, King João II, and King Manuel I, architects of the system that commodified Africans and scattered their descendants across continents. And although they looked purely European, blood from Madragana flowed through their veins.

The chronicles of Gomes Eanes de Zurara describe what happened in 1441 with disturbing pride. On one voyage, Antam Gonçalves and Nuno Tristão captured a lone man and then a Black woman, referred to dismissively as a "Mooress." On the next, they took ten more, including Adahu, a local chief of the Azanaghi people. Adahu's nobility stood out. He communicated in Arabic through an interpreter, debated with his captors, and struck a bargain: if he were returned to his homeland, he would deliver other captives in exchange. Gonçalves agreed. The Portuguese returned in 1442 and collected ten new enslaved Africans as payment.

What began as ransom raids hardened quickly into commerce. In 1444, Portuguese forces staged a full-scale attack on Arguin Island, capturing 240 men, women, and children. Zurara reports that they were paraded naked on the docks of Lisbon. The crowd, he wrote, marveled at the sight. The Portuguese crown had discovered a new kind of treasure—not gold but people.

This is where Madragana and Adahu meet, not in person, but in legacy. Madragana's descendants sat on the throne when Adahu and the first twelve were seized. Her bloodline helped authorize the very expeditions that set the transatlantic slave trade in motion.

The irony is staggering. Europe's royal families carried the blood of a Black noblewoman yet treated other Black people as less than human. They did not see the connection or perhaps chose not to. Madragana's own kin, distant cousins, descendants of her homeland, were captured, branded, and sold.

This contradiction undercuts a foundational myth of Europe: that its ruling houses were racially pure, defenders of a "Christian" identity untainted by Africa. In truth, one of Portugal's earliest royal mothers was African. And yet her legacy was twisted, used not as a bond but as a justification to enslave millions.

Historians often debate the roles Africans and Europeans each played in the transatlantic trade. Yes, African leaders sometimes sold captives to Europeans, often prisoners of war or people enslaved under local systems of servitude. But European involvement transformed what had been limited and circumscribed into something entirely different: punishment in perpetuity, racialized and globalized.

When Africans participated in capturing other Africans, it was often within a framework of clan rivalries and obligations. When Europeans arrived, they imposed an external market that treated Africans not as temporary dependents or prisoners but as commodities. The distinction is not trivial. One was bound by context and custom; the other by a profit calculus that consumed generations.

The cruel irony deepens here, too. For Europeans, the Africans they captured looked different. Yet through Madragana, their own genealogy was entangled with Africa. They were, in effect, enslaving the kin of their own royal ancestor.

The stories of Madragana and Adahu remind us that history is never neat. It is tangled, intimate, and often contradictory. The same dynasty that claimed racial purity was built on the union of a Black Muslim woman and a Christian king. The same princes who charted the seas charted the mass movement of bodies in chains.

Remembering Madragana forces us to see Europe's royal houses not as sealed-off bastions of whiteness but as families already indebted to Africa. Remembering Adahu and the first twelve lets us pinpoint the moment Europe chose to build wealth on flesh.

Today, as debates rage about reparations, the legacies of slavery, and the unacknowledged African ancestry in Europe's own nobility, these stories demand attention. They complicate the narrative of "civilization" and "progress." They reveal that the very foundations of Western power were built on contradiction: honoring a Black woman as the mother of kings, while condemning millions of her kin to servitude.

History loves its ironies. Few are as haunting as this: Madragana, a Black noblewoman whose blood flowed into Europe's royal houses, became the matriarch of a dynasty that enslaved her own people. Adahu, one of the first twelve, was both victim and negotiator, a man whose captivity marked the beginning of a catastrophe that would uproot millions.

Together, their legacies expose the hypocrisy at the heart of Europe's rise. For every palace built on exploration, there were chains. For every celebration of noble lineage, there was silence about its African root. And for every chronicle that praised "discovery," there were voices like Adahu's, bargaining for freedom on a shore that would soon echo with the cries of the stolen.

To tell their stories side by side is not to collapse them into a single tale but to show the entanglement of bloodlines and betrayals. Europe's kings claimed nobility while practicing barbarism. And a Black woman's descendants helped inaugurate an empire of slavery that would scar the world for centuries.

THE FORGOTTEN STORIES BENEATH THE STADIUMS

In 2023 and 2024, I made two pilgrimages to Bank of America Stadium in Charlotte, North Carolina, to see the Carolina Panthers play football. I met my family halfway in Danville, Virginia, and together we drove the two-plus hours south. My father, retired from the Virginia Department of Corrections and battling bone cancer, wanted to make memories with his sons—memories untouched by hospitals, appointments, or the slow encroachment of time.

He spared no expense. Lower bowl seats, close enough to see the players' faces and feel the pulse of the crowd. I'd been to other games before—the SEC Championship at the Georgia Dome, NBA playoffs, even a Washington Commanders preseason matchup—but nothing compared to the electricity of stepping out of the tunnel and into the blinding expanse of that Carolina stadium. The field opened up like a green dream.

Though I remained loyal to the Commanders, I rooted for the Panthers those days. The concessions reminded me I was deep in the South: Bojangles, Krispy Kreme, Coca-Cola. The Panthers lost both games, against the Cowboys in 2023 and the Chiefs in 2024, but the 2024 matchup came down to a last-second field goal. For a few hours, we lived only in the moment.

Then, months later, I stumbled upon a story that hollowed me out. In 1913, at the site where Bank of America Stadium now stands, a Black man was lynched. I read the account again and again, struggling to absorb the weight of it. I pictured a mob gathered in that same place, roaring—perhaps with the same ferocity we now reserve for touchdowns. I wondered if his body hung there for days. I wondered if his family ever saw justice or if they were simply left to bury their grief in silence.

Then another layer surfaced. Bank of America, whose name crowns the stadium, issued a formal apology in 2005 for its predecessor institutions' ties to slavery. Banks like Boatmen's Bank and the Bank of Metropolis—now absorbed into Bank of America—once accepted enslaved people as collateral. Some even took ownership of them when debts went unpaid.

The irony was staggering: a stadium where Black athletes perform for tens of thousands, financed by a corporate legacy rooted in bondage, built atop ground soaked in racial violence. Over 110 years later, the same soil that bore witness to terror now fuels Charlotte's economy through sports and entertainment.

And yet most fans, myself included, cheered, drank beer, and sang fight songs without ever knowing the full story beneath our feet.

The realization didn't erase the joy of those memories with my father. But it complicated them. It reminded me that in America, celebration and sorrow often occupy the same ground—even the same breath. We are constantly walking on haunted earth, playing, building, and winning atop histories we've never fully reckoned with.

How many other stadiums sit atop erased histories? How often do we celebrate without remembering what the ground has already endured?

When cities spend hundreds of millions in taxpayer money on stadiums, they are not only making bets on economic development. They're making decisions about whose histories are paved over and whose futures are funded. Again and again, these choices benefit sports owners and developers at the expense of working-class communities, often Black and brown ones, whose ties to the land run deeper than any deed.

In Washington, D.C., the area surrounding RFK Stadium borders Kingman Park and Hill East—neighborhoods long redlined, now rapidly gentrifying. And before RFK, that land was adjacent to plantations owned by men like Notley Young, a major D.C. landholder and enslaver. Today, Nationals Park, hailed for revitalizing the Navy Yard, stands on ground where Black people were once bought, sold, and worked to death.

In Northwest Stadium, in Prince George's County, Maryland—the current home to the Washington Commanders—lies in a county once dominated by tobacco plantations and Black tenant farmers. The NFL team may have changed its name, but the soil beneath the cleats remains steeped in injustice.

In Tampa, Tropicana Field sits on what was once the Gas Plant District, a thriving Black community of homes and businesses. Over one hundred

Black families were displaced to make room for the stadium, promised a return that never came. The site may also contain burial grounds linked to Black churches—something city officials admitted they may never fully investigate.

In Jacksonville, TIAA Bank Field was partially built on the Old City Cemetery, where Black residents, including formerly enslaved people, were buried. In Houston, Minute Maid Park looms near Freedmen's Town, a once-thriving Black neighborhood born from emancipation. In New Orleans, the Caesars Superdome obliterated Backatown, a community with roots in slavery and Reconstruction.

In the 1950s, Los Angeles seized Chavez Ravine to build Dodger Stadium, displacing a Mexican American community with promises of public housing that never materialized.

The University of Texas's stadium sits on land once granted for westward expansion and slaveholding.

This isn't a call to tear down stadiums. It's a call to acknowledge what lies beneath them. Because every touchdown scored, every anthem sung, every dollar made in these places echoes with a deeper question: What lies below?

Until we answer that, the games we play will always be shadowed by the graves we ignore.

SERVED BY MY KIN

The Strange Privilege of Black Tourism

I travel about once a year, not to escape who I am, but sometimes to better understand it.

In Jamaica, the Bahamas, Aruba, and Curaçao, I've found pieces of myself, echoes of language, rhythm, and skin tone that feel achingly familiar. The Caribbean is where the African diaspora wears sunlight on its shoulders. But for all the joy these places bring me, there's also something heavier: the quiet discomfort of being a Black American served by Black hospitality workers in nations shaped by slavery and empire.

The Caribbean economy was built on extraction, first sugar, then bauxite, now tourism. What's changed is the currency, not the structure.

Today, the region's primary export isn't a crop but an experience. Paradise has become a product, and the labor force selling it is overwhelmingly Black. In Jamaica, St. Thomas, the Bahamas, Turks and Caicos, and elsewhere, locals manage the beaches, pour the drinks, cook the food, and staff the resorts. The clientele is often white, increasingly Asian, and, in growing numbers, Black American.

As a Black tourist from the United States, I exist in a strange space: racially aligned with the staff, class aligned with the guests. The dissonance is striking. The people serving me could be cousins, or might have been, had the transatlantic slave trade charted a different route. Their ancestors were enslaved on Caribbean plantations; mine, on American ones. Now, generations later, I come to their land to rest, and they bring me towels, clean my room, and wish me a pleasant stay.

Sometimes I over-tip, hoping to soften the imbalance. I greet staff warmly, ask about their families, and make small talk. But none of that changes the reality: I have leisure; they have labor. And while many are justifiably proud of their work, the power dynamic echoes something older and more sinister. The plantation may be gone, but its architecture lingers in the tourism industry.

I always try to carve out time from the beach to visit a local museum or historic site. The stories, though varied, follow familiar arcs: Indigenous people pushed out, Africans brought in, enslaved people worked until emancipated—or until they overpowered their oppressors. In Bermuda, I saw Black people with British accents, the voice of their colonizer. In Jamaica, I met men named Winston and women speaking "likkle" this or that, the Irish echoing in their slang.

Sometimes I feel proud, seeing Black people employed, navigating an economy with limited options. Other times I feel trapped in a loop, watching an echo of servitude that now pays wages but still positions Black people as helpers, often for foreign guests.

What does it mean to be free if the options are still shaped by the past?

The Caribbean is not monolithic. These islands hold innovation, culture, resilience, and pride. But I wonder how often we, especially Black Americans, engage with these places as more than vacation backdrops. Do we see the history beneath the hospitality? Do we question who owns the land under our resort? Who gets displaced for a new hotel? What wages are paid behind those smiles?

This is not to denigrate tourism. For many Caribbean countries, it's one of the few viable sectors left, especially where agriculture has withered or manufacturing never took root. Tourism brings relatively stable jobs, opportunities for tips, and even international exposure.

But we must interrogate the broader system. Why are so many nations still economically dependent on serving others? Why is the most reliable income source rooted in smiling subservience?

The plantation never disappeared. It evolved. From cane to cocktails. From overseers to operations managers. The vocabulary changed, but the labor dynamics remain hauntingly familiar.

To be clear, the answer isn't to stop traveling. The answer is to travel with consciousness and to support systems that empower, not just employ. That redistribute, not just reward. That see Black people not only as laborers of the sun but as owners of the soil.

To travel as a Black person in a Black-majority nation is not the same as a white tourist arriving with unconscious entitlement. But that doesn't make the dynamic simple.

I carry my passport and my privilege in the same pocket. And with every trip, I try to carry a little more awareness, too.

THE BERRY HILL MEGASITE WAS MOVED TO AVOID DISTURBING HUNDREDS OF ENSLAVED PEOPLE'S GRAVES

as appeared previously in Cardinal News

What is now a promising industrial site in Pittsylvania County was once a plantation where enslaved people labored before the Civil War. Here's a look back at the history.

Just outside Danville headed on U.S. 58 west toward Martinsville, the Berry Hill Megasite sits a few miles off the main highway on Berry Hill Road. It promises to be a huge economic driver, as Danville and Pittsylvania County have already invested over $200 million into the development with over 3,500 acres available on thirteen different lots for potential companies' use.

The site is being considered by battery separator company Microporous and was previously shortlisted by Hyundai and Ford. Companies will be able to draw on a workforce from Virginia and North Carolina, as the site sits a few miles above the border with Rockingham County, North Carolina. Additionally, a new bypass being built will allow for easier access to the area.

When the Berry Hill Megasite was in the planning phases, a critical issue arose: The initial site plan would conflict with an area where more than two hundred enslaved people were buried. The new and the old were confronting each other. Eventually, an alternate site plan was developed without disturbing the enslaved people's graves, but it shed light on the past. There was another type of megasite at Berry Hill and the surrounding communities: forced labor camps, also known as plantations, that produced the cash crop of tobacco by enslaved people.

Growing up in Danville, I passed the Berry Hill highway marker on U.S. 58 on the way to church in Cascade every Sunday. I would see the marker, but I never asked what it meant and never thought twice about it until recently. Reexamining the highway marker, I deciphered a few facts, but I still was not able to understand that Berry Hill was also a plantation on an initial read. As the marker states, "Berry Hill is situated 5¼ miles to the south on the Dan River. The original portion of the main house was built in 1745 and there have been several additions. The property was used as a hospital for General Nathanael Greene's army during the spring of 1781, following the Battle of Guilford Court House."

The new Berry Hill has thirteen lots for companies to make their homes. In the past, neighboring Henry County and Pittsylvania County had more than thirteen major plantations, most of them owned by the Hairston family. The Berry Hill community (not to be confused with the Berry Hill plantation in Halifax County) collectively had three plantations: Berry Hill, Oak Hill, and Oak Ridge. Except for Oak Ridge, the other plantations were under the jurisdiction of the Hairston family, who controlled more than forty-five plantations in four states, including Virginia and North Carolina. Fueling those plantations was the labor force of more than ten thousand enslaved people.

Berry Hill

Built on 1,200 acres in 1745 by Peter Perkins on land his dad left him in his will, the Berry Hill plantation has become a symbol of a time that has gone with the wind. The house was made with local lumber and doubled as a hospital in 1781 after the Battle of Guilford Courthouse, and legend has it that the home was originally named Buryhill because of the large number of British soldiers who died and were buried in the area. The name was eventually fashioned to its current format of Berry Hill.

Berry Hill owner Peter Perkins's last will in 1818 freed his four favorite enslaved people. In addition to granting them freedom, he also gave them each "one good horse, one cow, one sow, 20 pounds of corn, and my blacksmith tools." I'm sure that gave the newly freed people a decent start, but it would have been ideal if they also received land.

Ruth and Robert Hairston eventually became the owners of Berry Hill. Ruth's husband, Robert, ultimately went to Mississippi to run a plantation, leaving Ruth to run the day-to-day of Berry Hill. I wonder if it was uncommon back then for women to lead a plantation, or if it was business as usual. From the enslaved people's perspective, I wonder if the overseers and field hands had the same amount of fear for Ruth as a woman, if they preferred her versus Robert, if they had more sympathy for her, or if they hated her all the same.

Generations of Hairstons and enslaved people worked at Berry Hill. A few paces down the road was another plantation owned by the family, Oak Hill.

Oak Hill

Samuel Hairston built Oak Hill in 1822, near Berry Hill. Unlike Berry Hill, Oak Hill was made of brick instead of lumber, also sourced onsite. Samuel Hairston was known as the wealthiest man in Virginia and one of the wealthiest people in the nation. He possessed land and enslaved people worth an estimated $5 million, equivalent to $131.5 million today. Additionally, he was reputedly the largest slaveholder in the South. His labor force in Virginia and North Carolina totaled 1,700 enslaved people.

The enslaved people at Oak Hill were prohibited from religious activities, so they clandestinely worshipped in the woods. They probably ran into runaways, free Blacks, and enslaved people from other plantations and, for a moment in time, were able to freely give praise to the greater power they believed in. One of the first things the enslaved people at Oak Hill did when they got their freedom was to build a church, Piney Grove Primitive Baptist. I later came to learn that the small church beside my grandfather's house that I paid no attention to was Piney Grove Primitive Baptist, hallowed ground for the newly freed African Americans.

In 1868, roughly three years after the Confederacy surrendered, an anonymous note was sent to Oak Hill Plantation owner Samuel Hairston advising him to evict his Black tenants or there would be a massacre, stating the following:

> *If you cant move them we can and everything else. So take warning while you have the opportunity. Those vilans that now live on the plantation shall*

> *be burnt to Death if they do not move and leave the state. We are able to carry out our designs we can do so and we will do so at an unexspected time to you. Remove them and nothing will be disturbed. Otherwise all will be in…ruin. We are many in number.*

Oak Hill didn't go up in flames until more than one hundred years later at the suspected hands of vagrants and drug addicts. I would come to learn later that my ancestor labored at Oak Hill.

OAK RIDGE

George Adams owned the Oak Ridge Plantation, just up the street from Berry Hill and Oak Hill. My mother's maiden name was Adams, and it came down the generations from George. As I'd done with the Berry Hill marker, I passed by Oak Ridge countless times in my life without knowing what it was. I just thought it was a big, nice, older house with a lot of land. I never knew my ancestor labored there.

According to the National Register of Historic Places, the house "is a two-story Greek Revival/Classical Revival frame residence built in the late 1830s or early 1840s and enlarged chiefly in the early twentieth century. The exterior features mostly beaded weatherboard siding, a metal-sheathed hipped roof, a brick foundation and chimneys, and a monumental Doric portico. The five-bay front elevation is dominated by the early twentieth-century portico which has four monumental columns that support a gable roof with a pediment."

Free African American cabinetmaker and carpenter Thomas Day provided a few pieces of furniture for Oak Ridge. Based out of Milton, North Carolina, just across the border, he came from an established family, was well-educated, and primarily dealt with high-end white clientele.

Enslaved people at Oak Ridge cared for twelve cattle, eight milk cows, four horses, and sixty pigs and produced 225 bushels of wheat, 300 bushels of oats, and 18,000 pounds of tobacco—the cash crop—annually. This was a huge amount of output but pales in comparison to the neighboring Hairston powerhouse with multiple plantations and thousands of enslaved people.

In 1860, there were 112 enslaved people at Oak Ridge between plantation owner George Adams and his son-in-law Dr. John Wilson, who married his daughter Emma. One of those 112 enslaved was my great-great-great-grandfather Flem Adams Sr. (1830–1914), who stood seven feet tall, wore a size 22 shoe, had to duck to pass through doors, and wore people's worn pants as cutoff shorts.

When Flem got his freedom in 1865, he went to work on the Oak Hill Plantation as a sharecropper. I wonder if Flem was evicted from the property after the anonymous note was sent to Samuel Hairston. He would have had to gather his wife, Martha Adams, and three sons, Flem Jr., Daniel, and George, and make a way. I wonder if they were temporarily housed with other Black people, slept in the woods, or were taken in temporarily by Piney Grove Primitive Baptist Church. Sometimes I wonder, what were Flem's dreams and goals? To be the best farmer? Best husband or dad? To stay alive? To find his unknown parents? When I meet Flem in the hereafter, I'm sure he will tell me all about it.

Berry Hill, Oak Hill, and Oak Ridge Plantations were major producers of tobacco, which my ancestor Flem learned to cultivate. Years later, Flem's great-grandson, World War II veteran Calvin Adams Sr., worked as a farmer and cultivated tobacco for profit. Calvin worked as a farmer until he retired in the 1980s, with skills that were passed down generations from Flem. Calvin was able to benefit from the trade Flem was forced to learn. I even helped Calvin, my grandfather, in a small way by picking up tobacco leaves as a six-year-old, but thank goodness I never had to experience the back-breaking "pullin' 'bacca" that my ancestors did. More than two hundred Adams family members gathered for our first family reunion post-COVID in August 2022, just a few miles from Berry Hill. We gathered a short walk from Piney Grove Primitive Baptist Church. We are the descendants of Flem Adams Sr.

Looking Forward

Times of the past were complex. Not all Black people were victims, and not all white people were victimizers. Free African American cabinetmaker and carpenter Thomas Day also owned fourteen enslaved people, which was reportedly not uncommon. My hope is that he was as sympathetic as possible to his own race and treated them well. Additionally, some of the Hairston slave owners freed some of their enslaved people before 1865. This typically would not go over well with the rest of the family and showed the complexities of the times in which they lived.

Today, Oak Ridge still looks beautiful, and people live there. However, the Berry Hill property is boarded up and looks condemned. The Oak Hill property is in ruins. There was a time when the properties were beautiful and the industry was ugly. Now these properties are ugly, and hopefully, the industries nearby will be fruitful.

Nowadays, Berry Hill won't be just known as a historic house, as a hospital for past soldiers, or as a community of forced labor camps for enslaved people. It will be known as an economic engine, a megasite that provides jobs for families and a home for companies. It may be an automotive plant, it may be something else, but thank goodness it won't be the site of humans working against their will for free. I'm sure the property will become the home to several companies in the next few years. Despite the history, good, bad, ugly, or whatever you may classify it as, the future of the *new* Berry Hill appears to be far brighter than the *other* Berry Hill. And I'm sure folks from the past, both slave owners and the enslaved, will become proud of what the area will be, unlike the sins of the past.

INDIGENOUS PEOPLE NEED A PERMANENT VOTING SEAT IN CONGRESS

as appeared previously in Medium

Indigenous people need more than a day; they need more than a month. Thank goodness they have those, but it's not nearly enough for their contributions and the disrespect they have taken. Their land was taken, they were forcefully relocated to reservations during the Trail of Tears, they were forcibly sent to boarding schools to *get the Indian out of the Indian*, and they were nearly exterminated as a race. America is not America without the forced sacrifices and contributions of Indigenous people. How do we make Indigenous people a priority in a land of partisan divisiveness, whitewashing of history, national debt, and pending international conflict? How do we focus on our Indigenous brothers and sisters every day and month of the year, not just their day or month?

In 2022, history was made for the first time in 230 years when an Alaska Native, Hawaiian Native, and Native American were elected to the U.S. House of Representatives. This is great, but sadly for 229 years, Indigenous people were not fully represented in Congress. Solution—one federal House and Senate voting member seat should be added specifically for Indigenous representation. The seats would be filled by a democratic vote of Indigenous Nations' citizens. Having guaranteed voting member seats at the table of lawmakers will at least ensure Indigenous concerns are heard regularly and reverberated in the lawmaking process. (It's important to note that in 2019 and 2021, the Cherokee Nation and United Keetoowah Band of Cherokee Indians were able to appoint non-voting members to the U.S. House of Representatives through the 1835 Treaty of New Echota with the U.S. government. Although appointed, the selected members have yet to be seated by Congress.)

In 1862, President Abraham Lincoln signed the Morrill Act, which reallocated land taken from Indigenous Nations to states to establish land grant universities. Solution—have land grant universities provide respective Indigenous Nations in their localities with regular payments. This solution wouldn't give the land back altogether but would at least acknowledge past wrongdoings and allow the Indigenous Nations to benefit financially, similar to a rental agreement with a tenant. There are over one hundred land grant universities in the United States, so the benefit to Indigenous Nations throughout the country could be exponential. Process-wise, university payments could go directly to the U.S. Bureau of Indian Affairs and would then be distributed to local Indigenous Nations.

Overall, it's been a long time since landmark dates in the nation's history of 1492, 1619, 1776, and 1865. A lot of mistakes were made at the expense of Indigenous folk. We can't reverse the past, but we can improve the present and future for our Native citizens. Adding seats to Congress and having land grant universities provide payments would be two huge critical steps for our Native citizens. Indigenous people need more than a month, and they definitely need more than a day. They need our commitment every day.

WILL ST. PAUL'S COLLEGE BOUNCE BACK LIKE MORRIS BROWN?

as appeared previously in Medium

In HBCU-fertile Virginia, St. Paul's College (SPC) was one of six colleges for Black people that formed after slavery. In addition to SPC (1888), Virginia State University (1882), Virginia Union University (1865), Hampton University (1868), Norfolk State University (1935), and Virginia University of Lynchburg (1886) were established to support education for Black students.

Over ten years since closing, SPC's legacy still endures. My best friend attended SPC in the mid-2000s. Two of my aunts attended SPC in the 1970s. One aunt played tennis and softball. Both aunts pledged AKA. My friend played football for the Tigers squad. I remember making a few trips to Lawrenceville, a small town about forty-five minutes west of Petersburg and just over an hour southwest of Richmond.

Although SPC closed in 2013, it didn't sell until 2017, when Xinhua Education Investment Corporation paid $2.5 million for it. Although Morris Brown College (Mo B) did not close its doors, it went through a similar journey of financial hardship. In 2002, Mo B—based in the Atlanta University Center with Spelman College, Morehouse College, and Clark University—lost its accreditation from the Southern Association of Colleges and Schools due to financial woes. From there, enrollment dropped significantly, and the university was on the verge of bankruptcy until investors stepped in.

Twenty years later, Mo B managed to gain full accreditation again by the Transnational Association of Christian Colleges and Schools.

Most recently, the nonprofit St. Paul's Leadership Institute was formed with the support of Virginia Tech through the Vibrant Virginia Initiative to establish professional development programs. As its mission states, the St. Paul's Leadership Institute "is devoted to creating an equitable, family-based academic environment that will produce well-prepared and empowered leaders for the challenges of the evolving world." In July 2023, the group taught leadership skills during a five-day series to students ages fourteen to eighteen. The nonprofit has long-term aspirations to purchase the campus.

Could it be possible to reopen SPC with partnerships at Virginia Tech, a potential renewed interest from St. Augustine's University, and the nation's renewed interest in diversity efforts post–George Floyd? If SPC were reopened, would students be interested in attending? Would it be a slow burn to build up enrollment? Is the brand forever tarnished and should it remain closed? Is Mo B enough of a case study to prove it possible? Let's also not forget, Virginia underfunded HBCU neighbor Virginia State University by $277 million. Could that money be awarded in the future and bring the St. Paul's campus under the Virginia State University umbrella? There are a lot of questions that we can ask, but it's clear there is still an appetite for higher education in Lawrenceville.

IT TAKES A VILLAGE

How the Black Community in Lexington Supported VMI and Its First Wave of Black Cadets

as appeared previously in Cardinal News

VMI accepted its first Black cadets in 1968. Here's how the Black community in Lexington supported them.

There's an African proverb that says, "It takes a village to raise a child." In this type of community, your neighbors treat you like family and pour into you with the same love as they have for their own children. For us folks in the Black community, that love also extended to administering punishment, but that's a topic for another day. As defined by professor and researcher Andrea Reupert, it

> *takes many people ("the village") to provide a safe, healthy environment for children, where children are given the security they need to develop and flourish, and to be able to realize their hopes and dreams. This requires an environment where children's voices are taken seriously and where multiple people (the "villagers"), including parents, siblings, extended family members, neighbors, teachers, professionals, community members and policy makers, care for a child. All these "villagers" may provide direct care to the children and/or support the parent in looking after their children.*

The twenty enslaved Africans (and I would argue all of the other enslaved Africans thereafter) who arrived in the Tidewater area of Virginia on August 20, 1619, brought the "village" ethos with them from the motherland. Just over 349 years later, four young men from the same area of Virginia as those Africans, in addition to one from Warrenton, left their villages to attend Virginia Military Institute (VMI) in the Shenandoah Valley of Lexington, Virginia. This wasn't just another college sendoff, though. On August 22, 1968, they became the *first* African Americans to attend the revered institution of higher learning, commonly referred to as the West Point of the South. (Ying-sing Wen from southern China was the first non-white cadet to matriculate, in 1904.)

So, what happens when young men grow up and leave the village? When they leave for a job or to attend college, do they then find another village?

The *New York Times* described Lexington (also home to Washington and Lee University) as a small liberal college town with Confederate roots. But what about the everyday folk in the town who support the universities? The generational Lexingtonians? The people who support those cadets either directly or indirectly? The people who *didn't* land in Lexington based on higher education, liberality, or confederating? What about the people who reside in the town and will be there long after the cadets are gone, long after they have ventured into their military or civilian careers? To these people, Lexington is not just a college town with Confederate roots; to them, Lexington is home.

The year 1968 was a pivotal one in the country's history, especially with the urgent push of the civil rights movement. As for Lexington in 1968, retired registered nurse and Lexingtonian Priscilla Baker was able to shed light:

> *Well, the first* [Black] *class, I'm sure maybe they didn't know exactly what they were coming to. Segregation wasn't as out there as in some places. But it was here in this area. But the community, the Black community really accepted the cadets. They came to church, they were invited to people's homes for meals, and they became friends with the people in the community.*

Historically, the Lexington Black community has supported VMI, mainly in domestic functions early on but then in roles of leadership as opportunities became available. Although the young men were no longer kids in the literal sense, the Lexington Black community still adopted them like one of their own. Not only were they welcomed at a surface level of pleasantries and well wishes, but they were also welcomed into the community pillars of the Lexington Black village: the Black church, Sunday dinner, and the Black barbershop. Not only did the community invest time in them when they were there, but those relationships stayed intact long after the young men were students.

Coming from a small town myself, I understand how the community becomes tightknit. Everybody knows everybody. And when new folks join our community, we tend to rally around them to make them feel welcome. If you are from a southern state and a small town, chances are people will ask you where you go to church. And if you don't have one, they'd be happy to welcome you to theirs. First Baptist Church of Lexington, the area's historic Black church since 1867, supported the young men also making history of their own.

Harry Gore, class of 1972 and the first Black person to be accepted to the Institute, shared his experience with the local community:

> *The Black people in Lexington were very welcoming and very accommodating. We went to First Baptist Church, which is right there on Main Street, and they welcomed us with open arms. The pastor at the time was a man named John E. Trotman, and he and his wife were very gracious to us. They had us over to their house for dinner most Sundays after church. And the Sundays that we didn't go to their house is because we're going to someone else's house.*

I'm sure the community wanted to welcome the young men they had heard about—the young men they had read about in the newspaper, saw news stories about on television, and heard about in the barbershop, beauty shop, church, and grocery store.

Baker continued, "I don't think we really had any apprehension about the cadets going to VMI. I mean, Black and white people in the community got along with each other. I'm sure they [VMI administration] were also on their Ps and Qs to make sure everything went okay."

As Dick Valentine '72, another member of the first class of Black cadets, mentioned in a previous interview with the *Washington Post*, their integration "turned out to be a non-event....In the Rat Line, everyone was treated [harshly], and you don't think it's racially motivated because the white guy next to you is getting it too."

I was curious about the relations among the different communities of Lexington, especially after the assassination of Dr. Martin Luther King Jr., but the white and Black Lexingtonians appeared to have an amicable relationship going back generations. First Baptist Church formed out of Manley Memorial Church, a church that supported white and Black (free and enslaved) worshippers alike.

Valentine continued, "There was a lot of curiosity about us in the town, and in the Black community, there was a lot of pride at finally seeing our faces in those uniforms."

A lot of Black families show love through meals and their cooking. "Sit down here and eat somethin'. We gotta put some meat on dem bones," my grandmother would say. I'm sure for the cadets, shared meals also served as a check-in, and when they became familiar with one another, I'm sure it was good for them to see familiar faces beyond campus. The challenges didn't stop when the rat line ended, so it was good for them to get a regular stream of encouragement from people who eventually became an extended family for them.

Baker mentioned that her mother-in-law, Marie Baker, hosted the cadets for meals after church. As a foodie, I asked her about the details of a typical Sunday meal: "Typical southern food. I mean, everybody likes fried chicken [commonly referred to as the gospel bird in the church community]. And then all the things that go with it. Mac and cheese, corn pudding, green beans, just a typical Sunday meal."

Pastor John E. Trotman, a North Carolina native and generous host of the cadets while pastoring First Baptist Church, grew up in a home with eleven family members, whom he says were all close. In a 1991 interview with the *Daily Advance* (North Carolina), he reflected on his upbringing and thoughts on role models:

> *We had one meal, at least, where everybody ate together and we would sit and talk. It brought parents and youngsters together....In my community, neighbors were your parents. Teachers would visit the house, so everyone raised us....Role model people are people that should be possessed with a fire to do whatever it takes to set a standard for young people.*

Growing up in that type of home and living the "village" example, it was natural for Reverend Trotman o take new cadets under his wing and spend time with them over a meal with his family. Not only him, but I'm sure the whole church community took ownership and prayed for them.

Baker recounted her "village" community of Lexington in a previous interview with the Historic Lexington Foundation:

> *Our neighborhoods were full of caring parents. I remember that the parents in my neighborhood were all very concerned with the safety and well-being of all the children. They watched out for each other's children and even went so far as to correct misbehavior of children other than their own. "We took care of each other": that is a phrase that's often heard when remembering those days and even now.... We have always attended church, and we belong to First Baptist. That place has been a very important part of our family life, and we still support it. We also hold a reverence for the little old Cedar Hill church* [deep in Rockbridge County], *which many of our older relatives attended.*

Baker continued, shedding light on the role of First Baptist Church in the cadets' tenure: "Church played a big part. And it's so funny when they got out of the rat line and got a break. At the church, we had breakfast for them when they first came. You would see them go to the phone and call home." (Rats historically have limited phone privileges.)

Gore also recalls when he and a few other cadets joined the Trotman family to watch Super Bowl IV. Kansas City beat Minnesota (twenty-five years before Patrick Mahomes was born). The meals and fellowship helped a lot: "It gave us a pep in our step to help us make it through the first part of the week."

Like meals, the Black barbershop can be an experience where you receive love and guidance. The barbershop can be therapeutic to customers, a place for men to go and blow off some steam among peers. From time to time, you may see the occasional eccentric personality (think *Coming to America*), but overall, it's a safe place where people try to help and advise the best they can. Some guys go to the barbershop to hang out and talk, even if they are not in need of a cut.

"After we got out of the rat line, when we could get downtown a little bit more often, we went to a Black barber, Wendell," said Gore. Wendell's barbershop served as a pillar in the community for nearly fifty years. Coincidentally, Wendell was married to Priscilla Baker until his passing in 2019.

As noted in the article "Heard It Through the Grapevine" about the historic importance of the Black barbershop:

> *The rise of Jim Crow laws limited spaces where Blacks could gather, and the barbershop filled this void, similar to Black churches but on a smaller scale.*

> *Further, "The barbershop is where Black men can come to reconnect, to be themselves, and enjoy each other's company," said Sean Thompson, owner of Sean's House of Masters Barbershop. "It's been called the Black men's country club. It doesn't matter how much you make, what your title is, we're all on the same level when we enter the barbershop. We laugh, we debate, we talk sports, and current events."*

In a previous interview with Historic Lexington Foundation, Wendell Baker recounted his journey as a barber:

> *I went to barber school in Washington, D.C., and then came back to Lexington to work for Dave Moore as a barber in the lobby of the Robert E. Lee Hotel, where I stayed for the next 10 years. Then I opened my own shop on Jefferson Street, and there I stayed for almost 50 years. On my days off, I went over to VMI to cut the hair of the cadets. I also had many friends at Washington and Lee, and often alums would return for a visit and come get their hair cut.*

Regarding his role as a barber and mentor, he stated, "I was sometimes a counselor. I would never repeat those things that were told to me. One day a man came in and he let me know that he was a friend of Mother Teresa. I said to myself, 'That's about as close as I'll ever get to sainthood!'"

His wife, Priscilla, would affirm, "And people would often say that he was like a therapist. And he would always tell them, what went on in the barbershop stayed in the barbershop." The barbershop was like Switzerland: a neutral, judgment-free zone.

One of Wendell's customers remembers him and the barbershop fondly:

> *For many of us it was a place we'd go to laugh, to share stories. There was always talk about whatever sport was in season. Some of us went there to learn, maybe something about life, something about the community perhaps we didn't know. At times he seemed to even be a therapist to some of us as he listened to our problems, more importantly, a friend.*

Phil Wilkerson '72, also a member of the first class of Black cadets, received support from the Lexington Black community. In a 2019 panel on the "History of Integration at VMI," he mentioned that the Baker family continued to support him beyond his cadetship. Wilkerson noted that Marie Baker would send him care packages even when he was stationed overseas in the military. It's because of the support of the Lexington Black community that he said he never felt alone while going through the challenges of VMI.

Wilkerson also noted during Parents Weekend that his family would stay with the Baker family. During the civil rights era, Black people had limited lodging choices (remember *The Green Book*?). Lexington had a few places to house Black lodgers, but people also stayed with local families they became acquainted with. They took care of each other.

As Priscilla Baker noted, "My mother-in-law and Ms. Wilkerson, they became really good friends. And we even visited their home in Hampton. And of course, they came to my mother-in-law's house. And they were best friends until Ms. Wilkerson passed first and then my mother-in-law passed."

Valentine, like the others, was also embraced by the community. However, he was fortunate enough to not only leave Lexington with a degree in engineering and lifelong relationships, but he also connected with his future wife. As Priscilla Baker noted, "In fact, a couple of them, I think, married local girls."

The cadets not only received encouragement off campus from the Lexington community, but they also received encouragement from Black staff on campus. Despite not being able to attend as students until 1968, African Americans have been involved with VMI in some capacity or another since its founding in 1839, primarily in domestic capacities, such as stoopies (trash pickup), laundry workers, and mess hall waiters. The Black staff at VMI all gave encouragement to the young men. Whether a nod, a cheerful greeting, or a quick check-in, staff was there to help in whatever capacity they could.

As the years passed, the relationship with First Baptist Church not only continued to develop with cadets, but it also developed with other members of the Institute. In the mid-'80s, while Reverend James Scott lived in Staunton and pastored at First Baptist, the parsonage was rented to a military officer on assignment at VMI. When Reverend Scott resigned in 1985, Air Force Chaplain Johnny Stewart, stationed at VMI's ROTC Department, served as interim pastor for over a year while the church sought its next permanent pastor.

Eventually, the number of minority cadets at VMI grew, and out of that growth came the formation of a student organization focused on African Americans, the Promaji Club. As Kendra Delahunt explains in her master's thesis:

> *On April 24, 1975, 18 Black cadets, under the leadership of Cadet Frank P. De Laine Jr. '76, submitted a permit to Superintendent Major General Richard L. Irby to found the Promaji Club. The club, with the backing of the Main Street First Baptist Church of Lexington (the very same church that provided VMI's first Black cadets with support), would be a club oriented toward community engagement and service. While not officially deemed a Black Student Union, the club would serve predominantly as a space for Black cadets, though all members of the Corps were welcome to join. The word Promaji was selected intentionally and means "togetherness" in Swahili. As its founding permit explains, Promaji was to "*[strive]* for the solidification of the bond of hospitality and goodwill between Black cadets and an extremely* [gracious] *Lexington community" and was to "act as a communicating body facilitating rapport among the community, Corps of Cadets, and the Institute."*

This further shows the continued support over the years of the First Baptist Church community and the village/togetherness fabric built into the student organization.

Although church for cadets is not mandatory as it once was in the '60s and '70s, the relationship between the First Baptist Church community and VMI cadets is still present today. The Reverend McKinley Williams, the current pastor of First Baptist Church, shared the following:

> *First Baptist Church is central to the success and well-being of many students, especially the VMI cadets. As the oldest independent African American congregation in the region, First Baptist Church of Lexington has always and continues to be a refuge for those whom the society deems as different. Currently, First Baptist Church has an open door for the cadets. Our church has a program where we get to know the cadets and share a meal with them. We have been encouraged by the cadets utilizing their skills to help renovate, paint, and clean the church. We also have had the cadets trim the greenery outdoors. We have had the Glee Club to provide the music for several Worship Services. Still, many members have invited cadets to their homes for food and fellowship.*

Former cadets in the first wave of Black students have also poured back into the VMI community. Mac Bowman '73, MD, and Eugene Williams '74 have both served at the highest level of the Institute, the VMI Board of Visitors. Williams, who was in the third class of Black cadets at VMI, also became the first Black Board of Visitors member at VMI in 1978. He operates the nonprofit College Orientation Workshop, a month-long summer program at VMI that exposes minority males in high school to life skills, academic development, college and career planning, and cultural enrichment. From their times as cadets being welcomed into the Lexington community to pouring back *into* the community years later, they have become part of the extended village.

So, why did the Black Lexingtonians welcome these early cadets into their village? Maybe they gave them love because they felt like they had newfound ownership in the VMI process. Up until that time, they couldn't attend. VMI was a place that existed in their community but wasn't for them. They could get a job in a labor-intensive role but not in the educational process. But then, the first waves of Black cadets provided hope. Those in the community could cheer for the school now for cadets who looked like them.

There are aspects of VMI that may not have helped its relationship with the Black community historically; however, VMI continues to show progress over time. Dick Valentine said it best: "We can talk about things we hate and things we want to see different about VMI, but that's because we love it." (This is similar to me as a sometimes disgruntled yet diehard Washington Commanders fan.)

Maybe Black Lexingtonians were excited to have more people who looked like them in town, so they wanted to be hospitable and show their appreciation. The concept of Black people being allowed to attend VMI as students was new, but the concept of Black people welcoming newcomers into the community was and is commonplace. Business as usual. Not that it didn't mean anything; it means a lot. Especially in a land where we are the minority. But the concept of the village, that togetherness, came with us from the motherland.

Mark 12:31 says, "Love your neighbor as yourself." The Black people in Lexington exemplified and lived that. Maybe the cadets were welcomed into the community for all of the reasons mentioned; but at the core, I think it goes back to that African proverb, "It takes a village to raise a child." From the first Black cadets, the first female cadets, and the first Black Board of Visitor members to Major General Wins, the first Black superintendent, the Black community of Lexington has embraced, prayed for, and supported Black people on the inside of VMI every step of the way.

BLACK BASEBALL MATTERS, TOO

as appeared previously in Danville Register and Bee

Recently, Major League Baseball added Negro League stats to its record books, something that is long overdue.

Like the pro leagues, unfortunately, most localities at the prep level also had separate leagues for Blacks and whites during the Jim Crow period. The Danville area was no exception. Despite the separation, the Danville region was a talent-rich area for prep baseball, with multiple state championships as proof.

The George Washington Eagles, previously known as the George Washington Cardinals, amassed an amazing five state championships during the segregated years. According to the Virginia High School League record book, they won baseball state championships in 1926, 1928, 1931, 1953, and 1954. Unfortunately, World War II put a pause on the state baseball tournament from 1939 through 1948, and it was further canceled from 1949 until 1952, so it's possible they would have won more championships during that time.

Not to be outdone, the Langston Lions, the city's Black high school, won two baseball state championships in 1957 and 1964. I'm sure Black students in the '20s and '30s had the talent, but access to opportunities and extracurricular activities was limited during that time. The 1957 team featured future hall of fame basketball coach Harry Johnson. The 1964 team featured C.B. Claiborne, who became the first Black basketball player at Duke University.

The '50s were clearly the golden area for prep baseball, with three combined state championships for the city's prep athletes. It makes me wonder if integration had happened earlier, say the '30s or '40s, and civil relations were smooth among the races, how many more championships would Danville's high schoolers have won? In 2019, the 1953 and 1954 back-to-back state champions were inducted into the Danville Sports Hall of Fame.

Today, Black Danville natives still have a resounding impact on the sport. Most notably, Paul Gillispie, who played his prep ball at G.W. and college ball at the University of Virginia, currently serves as the senior vice president of scouting for the Cleveland Guardians.

The MLB's recent addition of Negro League stats was a great step to make baseball more inclusionary, and ultimately the sport will become better for it.

THE LEGACY OF BELLEVUE HILL REBUILT AND REIMAGINED

as appeared previously in Danville Register and Bee

In the late 1800s, Black people in Danville made significant progress in a short period after being emancipated. Black men served on the police force and in local politics, holding a majority presence in lawmaking in the city as members of the Readjuster Party. Unfortunately, the Danville Riot and events of Black voter suppression reversed the progress that was made, forcing Black people in Danville to turn inward, relying on their communities and God.

One such community was Bellevue Hill, located where O.T. Bonner Middle School is currently. Previously, it existed as a strong Black community with over fifty houses and families, and in 1889, six years after the Danville Riot, the Bellevue Hill Baptist Church was formed.

In the early days, the church operated out of a vacant home. In 1897, the property was purchased to build a church by trustees Garland Breedlove, J.J. Moore, and Baynus Watkins for two dollars (equivalent to seventy-six dollars today). Matthew 18:20 states, "For where two or three gather in my name, there am I with them." Indeed, when Breedlove, Moore, and Watkins gathered to purchase property to build a church, God was with them.

In a town of over 130 churches, Bellevue Hill Baptist Church—now Bellevue Missionary Baptist Church on Luna Lake Road—has survived and recently celebrated its 135th church anniversary in October 2024. Member Cathy Hubbard, also a descendant of Baynus Watkins, said during the 135th anniversary commemoration video, "I was raised on Bellevue Hill. And that's where Bellevue Church was established."

Genesis 9:7 states, "Be fruitful and increase in number; multiply on the earth and increase upon it." Most notably, founding trustee Baynus Watkins multiplied his flock, having eleven children with his first wife and an additional eleven kids with his second wife after his first wife passed away. His second wife, Kate, helped with all twenty-two kids and showed the same love to the first eleven as she did to her own. Various descendants of their family remain involved in the church today, with many in leadership roles.

Deaconess Francis Smith mentioned during the 135th anniversary commemoration video, "Bellevue Hill was a great church. We was a great community. If a person was sick, the missionary would clean their house."

Deacon Mike Bennett, also a descendant of Baynus Watkins, remembers when he was introduced to the Bellevue Hill community. "When my dad wasn't working at the mill, he would take me down to Bellevue Hill to help build the house when I was a boy. It was a Jim Walters house, where the frame was set, and you built out the inside," he said.

Other members of his family also lived in the community, as his grandmother, aunt, and uncle all had houses on the same road. Mike's grandfather and Watkins's son-in-law, John Bennett, a deacon at Bellevue and a builder, helped construct the community church with his sons. Unfortunately, like most towns in the 1960s, urban renewal came, and the church and community were taken through eminent domain to build O.T. Bonner.

More well-known examples of schools displacing Black communities in Virginia include the University of Virginia, Old Dominion University, and Christopher Newport University. For a junior high school displacing the Bellevue Hill community in small-town Danville, the displacement went unnoticed beyond the county. The church would need to be rebuilt again.

The church has weathered obstacles over the years. It has survived and been rebuilt and relocated multiple times over the years. During the Jim Crow era, the church was burned down. Whether this burning was a hate act or an accident is lost to history, but no challenge has ever stopped the community from staying together and moving forward.

Like for all churches, the pandemic presented a challenge. Bellevue had to stop in-person service. Then they met for service in the parking lot outside and then back in person, socially distancing with masks on. Services are also live-streamed on YouTube.

Most churches post-pandemic experienced a drop off in young people not returning, opting for the convenience of online attendance. However, at Bellevue, there is a presence of young members who still attend in person.

And you can hear babies cry during service, a sign of the future congregation. The church has bounced back from being burned and forcefully displaced and the pandemic and has increased its membership in a town with churches on every corner.

During the 135th church anniversary service, Deacon Ernest Harris said, "God ain't gonna leave us. And to celebrate 135 years—that's proof right there. He's kept us 135 years. I know he'll keep us another 135 years."

Bellevue is more than a structure, a group of structures or homes. It is more than a neighborhood. Bellevue is wherever two or more are gathered.

Like the Israelites in the Bible's Old Testament who had to rebuild the temple numerous times, the people of Bellevue also rebuilt and reimagined. The thread of the people remains the same, though—inherited resiliency. During the 135th church anniversary service, Pastor Braxton Braswell said it best: "We thank God for what he has done, what he is doing, and what he will continue to do."

WILL BLACK VIRGINIANS END UP ON RESERVATIONS?

In a 2004 interview with the *Washington Post*, Ricky Haynie of Haynie Farms in Virginia mentioned, "You know what my gravest fear for black people is? That we'll end up on reservations. That we won't own any land." The first Africans to arrive in Virginia in the early 1600s were displaced from their home communities. This would begin a long history of Black Virginians being forcefully displaced for centuries to come.

Most recently, ProPublica examined Black communities displaced by institutions of higher education in Virginia. Expanding more broadly statewide to include multiple categories of displacement, over a three-month period, each region in Virginia was examined for the total displacement of Black communities, such as Black neighborhoods, including businesses and religious organizations. Of 133 total jurisdictions in Virginia, 80 communities in 38 localities were noted as having Black communities that were displaced.

Primary drivers for displacement were urban renewal and racial incidents. However, even in death, Black people's graves were subject to gross displacement, desecration, and even removal of dead bodies by grave robbers.

Virginia displacement instances were grouped into the following eight geographic regions: Eastern, Hampton Roads, Central, Northern, West Central, Southside, Valley, and Southwest. During the urban renewal effort alone, an estimated 7,996 families of color were displaced in Virginia. Also discovered during research were areas referred to historically as "sundown towns," known as places where Black people may suffer harm if not out of town by sundown. Additionally, sundown towns coincide with census records that show sharp declines in Black populations or very few Black people noted.

In the Eastern region, one displacement was revealed when fifty Black families in Onancock were forced to leave in response to a race riot in 1907. Chincoteague is noted historically as a sundown town.

The Hampton Roads region suffered seventeen displacements, most notably from urban renewal, with Norfolk experiencing the brunt of the hit, with over four thousand families displaced. Additionally, the Naval Weapons Station in Yorktown displaced six hundred Black families in the Reservation community. Poquoson is noted historically as a sundown town.

The Central region of Virginia encountered fourteen displacements, with Colonial Heights noted historically as a sundown town. The Vinegar Hill community in Charlottesville was forcefully removed for development, resulting in the closure of more than thirty Black businesses and the displacement of over six hundred Black families. The Gospel Hill community was displaced for an addition to the University of Virginia Medical Center. In Richmond, the construction of Interstates 64 and 95 displaced over seven thousand residents in the Jackson Ward community. Further, in Richmond, grave robbers took newly buried bodies from Black cemeteries to supply Virginia Commonwealth University and other medical schools with cadavers.

In the Northern region, fourteen Black communities were displaced; notably, the Queen City community was removed to build the Pentagon, and the Willard community was displaced to build Washington Dulles Airport.

The West Central region revealed nine displacements. In Blacksburg, the previous Black community of Newtown was displaced by a fire station, commercial development to support Virginia Tech's increasing student enrollment, and road construction. In Roanoke, the Northeast and Gainsboro communities were razed to construct the Civic Center and Interstate 581, with over twenty-four churches, two hundred Black businesses, one thousand graves, and 1,600 homes affected.

In the Southside region, eight Black communities were displaced, with Fieldale noted historically as a sundown town. In Mecklenburg County, a Black cemetery was relocated to support the commercial development of a Microsoft data center. In Pittsylvania County, the Wilson Family Cemetery in the Callahan Hill community was cleared, and a house was built over it.

The Valley region suffered ten displacements of Black communities, with Elkton known historically as a sundown town. In Lexington, home to several

Confederate memorials, the historical burial ground for Black people was acquired by the city, and houses were built over the burials in the 1940s. Black remains were supposed to be relocated to the Evergreen Cemetery, but evidence of the reburials was never substantiated.

Finally, in the Southwest region, three Black communities were displaced, with Buchanan County, Clintwood, Grundy, Narrows, Richlands, Weber City, and Wise known historically as sundown towns. Bristol is a city that claims both Virginia and Tennessee as home. On the Virginia side, the Black Bottom community, also known as Front Street, was displaced through urban renewal. On the other side of the state line in Tennessee, fifty-nine families from the Five Points community were displaced. The coal mining industry supported several other Black communities in the Southwest region. When coal companies left town, people in those communities migrated to other areas to seek opportunities.

Beyond the data, Black communities served as safe places in uncertain times. Black communities statewide were critical, especially for the Southside region in the 1960s. In response to the Bloody Monday protests in 1963, Martin Luther King Jr. mentioned he had "seen some brutal things on the part of policemen all across the South, but very seldom, if ever, have I heard of a police force being as brutal and vicious as the police have been here in Danville, Virginia." For Danville native Mike Bennett, his community in Bellevue Hill, with over fifty Black homeowners, was a safe haven from external conflicts when growing up during the civil rights era. His father would take him to the Bellevue Hill community, where he bought land and worked to build out their Jim Walter–style shell house. His neighbors were blood relatives, with his uncle's house to the left, his grandmother's home to the right, and his aunt's house to the right of his grandmother's house. His grandfather, a builder, helped to construct the community church. When urban renewal arrived in the '60s, the community was not spared. The church had to be rebuilt in a new location, and all the homes, including the house that Mike watched his father labor at the mill to save up for and build out himself, were demolished.

It may not come as a surprise that so many Black communities in Virginia were displaced, as Virginia is rooted in the Confederacy, with Richmond as the headquarters of the Confederate States of America and Danville serving as the final Confederate capital. Additionally, Virginia reportedly has the most Confederate memorials in the nation, even going so far as to remove the Black community of McKee Row in Charlottesville in 1919 to install a statue of Confederate General Stonewall Jackson in

1921. One hundred years later, the statue was formally removed amid the Black Lives Matter movement.

Related in parallel to Black community displacements are the American Colonization Society (ACS) and Rosenwald Schools. Although outwardly the ACS was veiled as an antislavery effort to send Black people to Liberia to live freely from slavery, strong sentiments were that the initiative was rooted in removing free Black people to protect the institution of slavery. The white public felt that free Blacks would negatively influence enslaved people, believing that Gabriel Prosser's failed insurrection in Richmond and Nat Turner's insurrection in Southampton were aided by free Blacks. Operating from 1820 to 1866, the ACS sent an estimated 3,700 Black people (mostly free but some enslaved) from over 120 communities throughout Virginia to Liberia.

During segregation, over 380 Rosenwald Schools, educational institutions for Black students, operated throughout the commonwealth. After integration, 256 schools were demolished. These were resources that could have been repurposed for other uses, such as churches, businesses, or auxiliary community centers.

Despite the numerous displacements across the state, two of the oldest Black spaces remain intact. The Pocahontas Island (peninsula) community in Petersburg formed in 1752, fought off displacement efforts in the 1970s, and remains today. The Tucker Family Cemetery in Hampton remains undisturbed and houses the bodily remains of the firstborn African American, William Tucker, whose parents, Isabella and Anthony, landed in Hampton in 1619. Many locations have issued public apologies for their roles in displacing Black communities, and yet some Black communities are still fighting not to get displaced today. It remains to be seen if Black people will end up on reservations, but it would not be a surprise based on how Black people have been pushed around in Virginia since 1619.

THE LAND MY MOTHER LEFT ME

Upon my graduation from college in 2006, my mom gifted me her most cherished earthly possession: a parcel of her family's land in Pittsylvania County, Virginia. The land was given to her by her father, who worked the land as a farmer until he retired, as did his father and his mother's father. Now the family meets there occasionally for family reunions or to leave flowers at the family gravesite.

Two hours south of Richmond, Virginia, and forty-five minutes north of Greensboro, North Carolina, lies Danville, Virginia, known as the last capital of the Confederacy. It was also known for operating the Dan River Textile Mills and most recently for opening a new casino where the mill used to stand. Just outside Danville in Pittsylvania County, my family has owned land in the Brosville community for over one hundred years.

John Breedlove, my maternal great-great-grandfather, was born a slave in 1864. He bought his first property, a 22-acre tract of land, from a white man, G.T. Green, in 1904. He was forty years old, the same age I am now. In total, he was able to acquire 160 acres of land. Looking back on it, purchasing land back then seemed unthinkable, but this was not as uncommon among Blacks back then as I originally thought. After the Civil War, Blacks desired land for farming. By 1910, Blacks had been able to acquire 19 million acres of land.

When John Breedlove died in 1941, he owed creditors for the land he acquired. Selling part of the land would have been sufficient to pay off his debts. Instead, all the land was erroneously sold without the family's consent.

In 1943, my family appealed to the Virginia Supreme Court. The local court judgment was proved null and void, and my family was able to retain a fifty-acre tract, with the rest being sold to satisfy John's creditors.

In the court case record, it is written, "The real purpose of WH Gray [William H. Gray, the person attempting to take the land] was to sell all lands of John Breedlove, a colored man, in a prosperous section of Pittsylvania County." John got a posthumous win.

My family weren't the only Black people to encounter people trying to take their land. Up to 98 percent of Black landowners were divested of their land. My father lived with other Black people in the Bellevue Hill community of Danville. When he was fifteen in 1968, the city took the land through eminent domain because they said they needed to build a school. The displaced Blacks like my dad insist the city just wanted the land and didn't like that Black people had managed to settle on a prime area of the city. My dad's grandfather, a builder, helped rebuild a new Bellevue Baptist Church on Lenox Avenue, about a mile up the street from where Wendell Scott, the first Black NASCAR driver, lived.

Although Pittsylvania County assessed a value on my family's property, to me this land is priceless. The land is a spiritual experience. My family planted corn, kale (they called it creasy salad), green beans, turnips, tomatoes, and potatoes. They packed preserves. They harvested tobacco. They had pig roasts and shared food with the entire community. My mother gathered apples from the apple tree and made my favorite breakfast, fried apples.

As a child, I remember playing on the land in the red dirt and picking up tobacco leaves when other family members were doing the hard work of pullin' 'bacca. It was normal to me; I didn't know any better. I thought every kid had a grandma and grandpa with a farm oasis for them to run around. I remember the best grapes I had in my life came from the grapevine there. But watch out for the bees!

I heard tons of stories there with my family. Stories about back in the day. Stories about war. Stories about segregation, my grandmother making fermented wine for church communion, folks getting baptized in the creek or the river, stories about my great-great-grandfather being seven feet tall in the 1800s and wearing people's used jeans as cutoff shorts.

My family was lucky to retain their land. We had the first family reunion there post-pandemic last summer. It was great to be there. Over one hundred people attended. My mother was bed-bound in a nursing home at that point, so I told her all about it when I went to see her afterward. She passed a few months later in October and was buried on the land, resting along with her siblings and ancestors who had gone before her. Like my ancestors before me, I was destined to rest there before my son passed. Now I plan to rest with him where he is buried in Alexandria.

When I pass by the land now, where the house that my grandfather built still stands, I envision my mother on the front porch, rocking in the chair. She's holding my son, her only grandchild, Jaylen. And like with me when I was young, when she would say my name in a singsong-y way, *Jeffrey Lee, Lee, Lee, Lee, Lee, Lee, Lee, Lee*, she's doing the same thing with Jaylen. I see her rocking with my son, and she's singing, *Jaylen Levi, Levi, Levi, Levi, Levi, Levi.* On *our* land. On *God's* land.

ACKNOWLEDGEMENTS

Thank you to my Lord and Savior, Jesus Christ, for placing the calling on my life to write. Thank you to my son in heaven for giving me the courage to share my writing with others. Thank you to everyone at The History Press. Let's celebrate history!

BIBLIOGRAPHY

Part I

Afro American Civil War. "United States Colored Troops History—African American Civil War Memorial Museum." afroamcivilwar.org/united-states-colored-troops-history.

Against the Current: Life on the Eastern Shore (Rising Waters, Land Loss). Local, USA. Co-production of WHRO Public Media and WORLD, April 29, 2024.

Apple Podcasts. "Revisiting the Story of Mary Bowser: The Enslaved Civil War Spy." podcasts.apple.com/us/podcast/revisiting-the-story-of-mary-bowser-the-enslaved/id1609909822?i=1000637882638.

Archambault, Alan. *Black Soldiers in the Civil War*. Bellerophon Books, 1995.

Bennett, Lerone, Jr. *Ebony Pictorial History of Black America*. Vol. 1. Johnson Publishing Company, 1971.

Bernstein, Lenny. "California Drought Hits Farmers Hardest." *Washington Post*, February 10, 2014. www.washingtonpost.com/national/health-science/california-drought-hits-farmers-hardest/2014/02/0.

Black America Web. "Little Known Black History Fact: The Origins of Hockey." June 13, 2019. blackamericaweb.com/2019/06/13/little-known-black-history-fact-the-origins-of-hockey.

BlackPast. "The True Reformers Bank, 1888–1910." www.blackpast.org/african-american-history/true-reformers-bank-1888-1910.

Blackshear, Thomas. *The Selection of Breeding of Negro Slaves*. June 1830. read.amazon.com/?asin=B09LXFM178&_encoding=UTF8&ref=dbs_p_ebk_r00_pbcb_rnvc00.

Blackstock, Uche, MD. *Legacy: A Black Physician Reckons with Racism*. Viking, 2023.

Booth, Glenda. "Preserving African American Heritage: Gum Springs." Zebra, February 7, 2020. thezebra.org/2020/02/07/preserving-african-american-heritage-gum-springs.

Brockell, Gillian. "Before 1619, There Was 1526: The Mystery of the First Enslaved Africans in What Became the United States." *Washington Post*, September 9, 2019. www.washingtonpost.com/history/2019/09/07/before-there-was-mystery-first-enslaved-africans-what-became-us.

City of Alexandria. "George Henry, Enslaved Ship Captain." www.alexandriava.gov/sites/default/files/2023-12/AAHT-6-Captain-George-Henry.pdf.

Coates, Ta-Nehisi. *The Message*. One World, 2024.

Court Issues. "Modern Day Hockey Created by Blacks?" court.rchp.com/modern-day-hockey-created-by-blacks.

DHR. "State Historical Highway Marker 'First Baptist Church' to Be Dedicated in Petersburg." January 24, 2025. www.dhr.virginia.gov/press-release-posts/state-historical-highway-marker-first-baptist-church-to-be-dedicated-in-petersburg.

Doe, Charles, letter, February 22, 1850. Accession 38743, Personal Papers Collection, Library of Virginia, Richmond, Virginia. edu.lva.virginia.gov/oc/stc/entries/a-new-englander-described-danville-slaves-february-22-1850.

DTN Progressive Farmer. "America's Best Young Farmer & Ranchers." spotlights.dtnpf.com/abyfr/PJH%202014.cfm.

Ely, Melvin Patrick. *Israel on the Appomattox*. Alfred A. Knopf, 2005.

Encyclopedia Virginia. "Excerpts from Equal Suffrage: Address from the Colored Citizens of Norfolk, Va., to the People of the United States. Also an Account of the Agitation Among the Colored People of Virginia for Equal Rights. With an Appendix Concerning the Rights of Colored Witnesses Before the State Courts (1865)." encyclopediavirginia.org/entries/excerpts-from-equal-suffrage-address-from-the-colored-citizens-of-norfolk-va-to-the-people-of-the-united-states-also-an-account-of-the-agitation-among-the-colored-people-of-virginia-for-equal-rig.

———. "Petit Marronage in the Great Dismal Swamp." encyclopediavirginia.org/entries/petit-marronage-in-the-great-dismal-swamp.

Enslaved. "Enslaved by George Washington, Harry Washington Escaped to Freedom—and Joined the British Army." www.enslaved.org.

Fair Farms Now. fairfarmsnow.org/black-land-ownership-in-the-maryland-farming-community.

Foster, Thomas. "Sexual Exploitation of the Enslaved." Encyclopedia Virginia, February 17, 2022. encyclopediavirginia.org/entries/sexual-exploitation-of-the-enslaved.

Gates, Henry Louis, Jr. *The Black Church: This Is Our Story, This Is Our Song*. Penguin Press, 2021.

Graves, Lee. "Slaves and Indentured Servants Were Vital to Virginia's Colonial Beer-Making." *Virginia Craft Beer Magazine*, August 19, 2019. virginiacraftbeer.com/slaves-and-indentured-servants-were-vital-to-virginias-colonial-beer-making.

Griffith, Alva. *Pittsylvania County, Virginia Register of Free Negros and Related Documentation.* Heritage Books, 2007.

Harriott, Michael. *Black AF History*. Deyst, 2023.

Haygood, Will. "The Promised Land." *Washington Post*, October 3, 2004. www.washingtonpost.com/archive/lifestyle/magazine/2004/10/03/the-promised-land/5269d006-f4ac-44e0-ba9e-25d9c50c93c4.

Hine, Darlene, William Hine, and Stanley Harrold. *African Americans: A Concise History.* 2nd ed. Pearson Education, 2006.

History. "The First Black-Owned Brewery in the US." November 6, 2024. www.history.com/topics/black-history/the-spirit-that-built-america-a-cold-one-video.

Horwitz, Tony. "In the Deep Swamps, Archaeologists Are Finding How Fugitive Slaves Kept Their Freedom." *Smithsonian Magazine*, 2016. www.smithsonianmag.com/history/deep-swamps-archaeologists-fugitive-slaves-kept-freedom-180960122.

Institute for Advanced Technology in the Humanities. "Virginia Emigrants to Liberia." Dataset. Institute for Advanced Technology in the Humanities, University of Virginia, Charlottesville, Virginia. virginians-to-liberia.iath.virginia.edu/research/jefferson.

Jones-Rogers, Stephanie. *They Were Her Property: White Women as Slave Owners in the American South*. ale University Press, 2019.

Joyner, Leanna. "The Community of Formerly Enslaved People at Brown Mountain Creek." Appalachian Trail Conservancy, February 17, 2023. appalachiantrail.org/official-blog/brown-mountain-creek.

Katz, William Loren. *Black Indians: A Hidden Heritage.* Ethrac Publications, 1986.

Kilke, Stephanie. "A Golden Age: King Mansa Musa's Reign." *Northwestern Magazine*, Spring 2019. magazine.northwestern.edu/features/caravans-of-gold-fragments-in-time/a-golden-age-king-mansa-musas-reign.

Kmorrow. "Black Dog–White Dog." wp.csusm.edu/kmorrow.

Laird, Matthew. "Lumpkin's Jail." Encyclopedia Virginia. Virginia Humanities, December 7, 2020. encyclopediavirginia.org/entries/lumpkins-jail.

"Mary B. Peatross, et al., v. W.H. Gray, Assignee of Maggie H. Barker, et Al." Virginia Supreme Court Records, vol. 181, October 1, 1943. scholarlycommons.law.wlu.edu/va-supreme-court-records-vol181/89.

McCartney, Martha. "Virginia's First Africans." Encyclopedia Virginia. Virginia Humanities, December 7, 2020, encyclopediavirginia.org/entries/africans-virginias-first.

McClure, Phyllis. "Rosenwald Schools." Encyclopedia Virginia. encyclopediavirginia.org/entries/rosenwald-schools

Mitchell, Preston. "Dan Fields: Black Mountain KY/VA." Black in Appalachia, July 18, 2022. Video, 9:15. www.youtube.com/watch?v=GIlj9yzXWTk.

Mohamud, Naima. "Is Mansa Musa the Richest Man Who Ever Lived?" BBC Africa, March 9, 2019. www.bbc.com/news/world-africa-47379458.

Monticello. "Slavery at Monticello FAQs—Property." www.monticello.org/slavery/slavery-faqs/property/#:~:text=Thomas%20Jefferson%20freed%20two%20people,members%20of%20the%20same%20family.

Mount Vernon. "George Washington and Slave Teeth." www.mountvernon.org/george-washington/health/washingtons-teeth/george-washington-and-slave-teeth.

———. "George Washington's Distillery." www.mountvernon.org/the-estate-gardens/distillery.

———. "Ona Judge." www.mountvernon.org/library/digitalhistory/digital-encyclopedia/article/ona-judge.

———. "William (Billy) Lee." www.mountvernon.org/library/digitalhistory/digital-encyclopedia/article/william-billy-lee.

National Museum of African American History and Culture. "Consecrated Ground: Churches and the Founding of America's Historically Black Colleges and Universities." nmaahc.si.edu/explore/stories/consecrated-ground-churches-and-founding-americas-historically-black-colleges-and.

National Park Service. "Ona Judge Escapes to Freedom." www.nps.gov/articles/independence-oneyjudge.htm.

———. "Petersburg: Pocahontas Island Historic District." www.nps.gov/articles/pocaisla.htm.

———. "The St. Luke Penny Savings Bank." www.nps.gov/mawa/the-st-luke-penny-savings-bank.htm.

NPR. "The Remnants of One of the Nation's Oldest Black Churches Have Just Been Found." October 7, 2021. www.npr.org/2021/10/07/1043964120/colonial-williamsburg-remnants-of-one-of-the-nations-oldest-black-churches.

PBS. "George Washington's Runaway Slave Harry." The African Americans: Many Rivers to Cross. www.pbs.org/wnet/african-americans-many-rivers-to-cross/history/george-washingtons-runaway-slave-harry.

———. "The Secret Group That Planned an Insurrection Against Slavery." PBS Originals, 8:08. www.pbs.org.

Port Cities Bristol. "Slavery in Africa." www.discoveringbristol.org.uk/slavery/people-involved/enslaved-people/enslaved-africans/africa-slavery/#:~:text=Slavery%20existed%20in%20Africa%2C%20but,gold%20mines%20of%20West%20Africa.

Pulley, Richard Demone. "The Role of the Virginia Slave in Iron and Tobacco Manufacturing." Master's thesis, 1962. Richmond University. Paper 941. scholarship.richmond.edu/cgi/viewcontent.cgi?article=1952&context=masters-theses.

Research Department of the Association for the Study of Negro Life and History. "Free Negro Owners of Slaves in the United States in 1830." *Journal of Negro History* 9, no. 1 (1924): 41–85. doi.org/10.2307/2713436.

Ruane, Michael E. "Virginia Is the Birthplace of American Slavery and Segregation—and It Still Can't Escape That Legacy." *Washington Post*, February

9, 2019. www.washingtonpost.com/history/2019/02/06/virginia-is-birthplace-american-slavery-segregation-it-still-cant-escape-that-legacy.

Schneider, Gregory. "Virginia after the Civil War: The Former Slaves Who Helped Shape the State's Government." *Washington Post*, March 26, 2018. www.washingtonpost.com/news/retropolis/wp/2018/03/26/powerful-and-forgotten-how-freed-slaves-helped-shape-virginia-after-the-civil-war.

Sedale, McCall. "Harsh History: Is There Virginia Wine Without Slavery?" SOMM TV Magazine, November 30, 2013. mag.sommtv.com/2023/11/history-virginia-wine.

Spivey, William. "America's Breeding Farms: What History Books Never Told You." Medium, August 23, 2024. williamspivey.medium.com/americas-breeding-farms-what-history-books-never-told-you-6704e8b152a4.

Swift, Kaleigh. "Complicating the Black Relationship to Wine: Part 1." France 44, February 22, 2024. www.france44.com/f44-news/complicating-the-black-relationship-to-wine.

SXSW EDU. "Henry Louis Gates Jr. & Paula Kerger on Reconstruction: America After the Civil War." YouTube. Video, 59:23. www.youtube.com/watch?app=desktop&v=g5svdBw7J3o&t=917s.

Thach, Liz, MW. "A Brief History of Black Winemaking in the US." Decanter, February 24, 2023. www.decanter.com/wine/a-brief-history-of-black-winemaking-in-the-us-498177.

TheGrio. "Race War One: The Secret History of the National Slave Revolt." www.thegrio.com.

TODAY.com. "Here's the Incredible Story Behind the Nation's First Black-Owned Distillery." April 23, 2022. www.today.com/food/people/chris-montana-first-black-owned-distillery-du-nord-social-spirits-rcna25700.

Turyn, Noreen. "Uncovering Lynchburg's Dark History of Urban Slavery." WSET, February 1, 2024. wset.com/news/local/uncovering-lynchburgs-dark-history-of-urban-slavery-museum-5th-street-ramona-battle-ted-delaney-february-2024.

Tyler-McGraw, Marie. *An African Republic: Black & White Virginians in the Making of Liberia*. University of North Carolina Press, 2007.

Virginia Changemakers. "Ona Judge." edu.lva.virginia.gov/changemakers/items/show/355.

Virginia Slave Narratives. Applewood Books, 1938.

Washington, Booker T. *Up from Slavery*. Doubleday, Page, and Company, 1901.

Wikipedia. "African American Officeholders from the End of the Civil War Until Before 1900." en.wikipedia.org/w/index.php?title=African_American_officeholders_from_the_end_of_the_Civil_War_until_before_1900&oldid=1272193252.

———. "African American Slave Owners." en.wikipedia.org/wiki/African-American_slave_owners.

———. "Great Dismal Swamp Maroons." en.wikipedia.org/wiki/Great_Dismal_Swamp_maroons.

———. "Hampton University." en.wikipedia.org/w/index.php?title=Hampton_University&oldid=1271431621.

———. "List of Members of the United States Congress Who Owned Slaves." en.wikipedia.org/wiki/List_of_members_of_the_United_States_Congress_who_owned_slaves.

———. "Petersburg, Virginia." en.wikipedia.org/wiki/Petersburg,_Virginia.

———. "Pocahontas Island." en.wikipedia.org/wiki/Pocahontas_Island.

———. "Slave Breeding in the United States." en.wikipedia.org/wiki/Slave_breeding_in_the_United_States.

———. "William Lee (valet)." en.wikipedia.org/wiki/William_Lee_(valet).

———. "York (Explorer)." en.wikipedia.org/w/index.php?title=York_(explorer)&oldid=1270267686.

WikiTree: The Free Family Tree. "Moses Dickson (abt. 1824–1901)." www.wikitree.com/wiki/Dickson-1005.

Willis, Samantha. "The Departed and Dismissed of Richmond." Scalawag, August 5, 2019. scalawagmagazine.org/2019/08/black-graveyards.

Zurara, Gomes Eanes de, C. Raymond (Charles Raymond) Beazley, and Edgar Prestage. *The Chronicle of the Discovery and Conquest of Guinea.* Printed for the Hakluyt Society, 1896. archive.org/details/chronicleofdisco01zura.

Part II

Alleghany Journal. Obituaries, November 15, 2019. www.alleghanyjournal.com/obits/obit.php?action=3&id=9922.

Alonso, Johanna. "Virginia Disputes Claim That It Underfunded an HBCU." Inside Higher Ed. www.insidehighered.com/news/quick-takes/2023/10/10/virginia-disputes-federal-claim-it-underfunded-hbcu.

AP News. "Historian: Football Stadium Sits on Site of 1913 Lynching." September14, 2021. apnews.com/article/race-and-ethnicity-sports-lynchings-college-football-arkansas-6c62c86c7f6f62ef19a3a1323b39e1b3.

Balls-Berry, Joyce, Lea C. Dacy, and James Balls. "'Heard It Through the Grapevine': The Black Barbershop as a Source of Health Information." *Hektoen International: A Journal of Medical Humanities* 7, no. 3 (2015). www.ncbi.nlm.nih.gov/pmc/articles/PMC4749262.

Berry Hill Historical Marker. Historical Marker Database, last revised on November 11, 2021. www.hmdb.org/m.asp?m=66054.

Black in Appalachia. "Bristol." www.blackinappalachia.org/bristol.

Black in Lexington. "Wendell Baker Profile." YouTube. Video, 1:34. www.youtube.com/watch?v=_u7Upj3kqbg.

Blacksburg, VA. "St. Luke and Odd Fellows Hall." www.blacksburg.gov/community/arts-and-culture/blacksburg-museum-and-cultural-foundation/st-luke-and-odd-fellows-hall.

Britannica. "Treaty of New Echota." www.britannica.com/event/Treaty-of-New-Echota.

Brunswick Times-Gazette. "St. Paul's Campus Sold for $2.5 Million." December 5, 2017. www.brunswicktimes-gazette.com/news/article_0254f2a2-d9e7-11e7-a4a2-9f48be19f519.html.

Cameron, Brian, and Andrew Kahrl. "UVA and the History of Race: Property and Power." UVA Today, March 15, 2021. news.virginia.edu/content/uva-and-history-race-property-and-power.

Center for History and New Media, George Mason University. "Histories of the National Mall: Map of Notley Young's Plantation." mallhistory.org/items/show/29.

Cosel, Janice, and Laura Leffel. "A Case Study of Pocahontas Island: Resistance to Post-Impact Evacuation in a Historic Black Community." *Electronic Journal* 1 (1999). members.tripod.com/~Richmond_ESM/ej0103.html.

Crane, John. "Old Slave Cemetery Found at Proposed Berry Hill Mega Park Site." NewsAdvance.com, September 25, 2009. newsadvance.com/archives/old-slave-cemetery-found-at-proposed-berry-hill-mega-park-site/article_aa605bd2-d6cc-52b3-b90e-cfcc87f540d6.html.

Delahunt, Kendra. "Uncivil War: Integrating the Virginia Military Institute." University of Chicago, July 2021. knowledge.uchicago.edu/nanna/record/3234/files/Uncivil%20War%3A%20Integrating%20the%20Virginia%20Military%20Institute.pdf?withWatermark=0&withMetadata=0&version=1®isterDownload=1.

Encyclopedia Virginia. "Chinese Student at Virginia Military Institute." encyclopediavirginia.org/262hpr-9eda30894f7bb3.

Epstein, Reid J. "A Liberal Town Built Around Confederate Generals Rethinks Its Identity." *New York Times*, July 26, 2020. www.nytimes.com/2020/07/26/us/politics/lexington-va-confederate-generals.html.

"50 Colored Families Ordered to Leave." Black Virginia: The Richmond Planet, August 17, 1907. blackvirginia.richmond.edu/items/show/873.

Finn, Peter. "At VMI, Pioneers Recall Breaking Earlier Barrier." *Washington Post*, October 5, 1997. www.washingtonpost.com/archive/local/1997/10/05/at-vmi-pioneers-recall-breaking-earlier-barrier/bb370fde-f457-4fc1-8249-e09a3e1395ff.

Firefli. "History of Integration Panel." VMI Alumni Agencies, May 1, 2019. www.vmialumni.org/history-of-integration-panel.

FOX 13 Tampa Bay. "Gas Plant District in St. Pete: One of the Oldest Black Neighborhoods Razed for Baseball." July 14, 2021. www.fox13news.com/news/

gas-plant-district-in-st-pete-one-of-the-oldest-black-neighborhoods-razed-for-baseball.

Gendreau, Henri. "Decades After Urban Renewal Razed Black Neighborhoods, Roanoke Prepares to Apologize." *Roanoke Rambler*, December 19, 2023. www.roanokerambler.com/decades-after-urban-renewal-razed-black-neighborhoods-roanoke-prepares-to-apologize.

The Guardian. "Bank Admits It Owned Slaves." December18, 2005. www.theguardian.com/world/2005/dec/18/usa.

Haygood, Will. "The Promised Land." *Washington Post*, October 3, 2004. www.washingtonpost.com/archive/lifestyle/magazine/2004/10/03/the-promised-land/5269d006-f4ac-44e0-ba9e-25d9c50c93c4.

Historical Marker Database. "Pocahontas Island Historical Marker." Last revised February 2, 2023. www.hmdb.org/m.asp?m=88809.

Historic Jacksonville. "A Walk Through History: Old City Cemetery." historicjacksonville.org/a-walk-through-history-old-city-cemetery.

History and Social Justice. "Virginia Archives." justice.tougaloo.edu/location/virginia.

Houston Chronicle. "Construction Damages Bricks from a Historic Houston Black Community." February 15, 2023. www.houstonchronicle.com/news/houston-texas/article/construction-damages-historic-houston-bricks-17804129.php.

Institute for Advanced Technology in the Humanities. "Virginia Emigrants to Liberia." Dataset. University of Virginia, Charlottesville, Virginia. virginians-to-liberia.iath.virginia.edu/research/jefferson.

Kellam, Brandi, and Louis Hansen. "Erasing the 'Black Spot: How a Virginia College Expanded by Uprooting a Black Neighborhood." Virginia Center for Investigative Journalism, September 5, 2023. vcij.org/urpooted.

Kelly, Devyn. "Black Businesses of Bristol." ArcGIS StoryMaps, May 1, 2020. storymaps.arcgis.com/stories/8dd5e7bc3bca4af5b0e707ac83bded9a.

Kennedy, Barbara. "Queen City: The Lost Black Community Swallowed Up by the Pentagon." BBC, June 19, 2024. www.bbc.com/travel/article/20240619-queen-city-the-lost-black-community-swallowed-up-by-the-pentagon.

KUT Radio, NPR. "Rediscovered Slave Quarters in West Campus Help Tell the Story of Urban Enslavement in Austin." February 18, 2022. www.kut.org/austin-news/2022-02-18/rediscovered-slave-quarters-in-west-campus-help-tell-the-story-of-urban-enslavement-in-austin.

The Lemur: Duke's Big Ideas Magazine. "The Dark Heart of Dodger Stadium: The History of Chavez Ravine." Duke University. lemur.duke.edu/the-dark-heart-of-dodger-stadium-the-history-of-chavez-ravine.

Mamon, Matt Busse, Grace. "Report: Manufacturer Eyes Pittsylvania County for $100 Million Investment." *Cardinal News*, November 28, 2023. cardinalnews.org/2023/11/28/report-manufacturer-eyes-pittsylvania-county-for-100-million-investment.

"Mary B. Peatross, et al., v. W.H. Gray, Assignee of Maggie H. Barker, et Al." Virginia Supreme Court Records, vol. 181, October 1, 1943. scholarlycommons.law.wlu.edu/va-supreme-court-records-vol181/89.

McGowan, Elizabeth. "Two Virginia Cities Aim to Reconnect Neighborhoods Isolated by Long-Ago Highways." USC Center for Health Journalism, July 26, 2023. centerforhealthjournalism.org/our-work/insights/two-virginia-cities-aim-reconnect-neighborhoods-isolated-long-ago-highways.

National Archives. "Morrill Act (1862)." August 16, 2021. www.archives.gov/milestone-documents/morrill-act.

National Institute of Food and Agriculture. College Partners Directory. www.nifa.usda.gov/land-grant-colleges-and-universities-partner-website-directory.

National Park Service. "Oak Ridge." National Register of Historic Places, June 29, 2017. npgallery.nps.gov/GetAsset/15e5a21e-90b7-4eee-b57c-aed08ae45e01.

Newkirk, Vann R., II. "The Great Land Robbery." *The Atlantic*, August 12, 2019. www.theatlantic.com/magazine/archive/2019/09/this-land-was-our-land/594742.

PBS. "Raised/Razed." Video. 58:00. www.pbs.org/video/raisedrazed-bg0gek.

Portugal Dicionário Histórico. "Biography of Alfonso III King Portugal 1210–1279." www.arqnet.pt/dicionario/afonsoiii.html.

Preservation Virginia. "Rosenwald School Architectural Survey." preservationvirginia.org/our-work/architectural-rosenwald-school-survey.

Reupert, Andrea, Shulamith Lala Straussner, Bente Weimand, and Darryl Maybery. "It Takes a Village to Raise a Child: Understanding and Expanding the Concept of the 'Village.'" *Frontiers in Public Health* 10 (March 11, 2022): 756066. doi.org/10.3389/fpubh.2022.756066.

Sabella, Anthony. "Four Descendants of the Reservation to Speak at Hampton History Museum Black History Month Presentation." News 3 WTKR Norfolk, February 4, 2024. www.wtkr.com/news/black-history-month/four-descendants-of-the-reservation-to-speak-at-hampton-history-museum-black-history-month-presentation.

Scheel, Eugene. "Dulles Airport Has Roots in Rural Black Community." History of Loudoun County, Virginia, November 2002. www.loudounhistory.org/history/dulles-airport-history.

Shivaram, Deepa, and Kyle Stewart. "Virginia Has the Most Confederate Memorials in the Country, but That Might Change." NBC News, June 9, 2020. www.nbcnews.com/news/us-news/virginia-has-most-confederate-memorials-country-might-change-n1227756.

SPC4LIFE: Reimagining St. Paul's. "SPC4LIFE: Reimagining St. Paul's College." spc4life.org/about.

St. Louis American. "Bank of America Apologizes for Role in Slavery." July 20, 2020. www.stlamerican.com/business/local_business/bank-of-america-apologizes-for-role-in-slavery/article_d5b8db38-c9e8-11ea-93fc-c78c5de5e8af.htm.

"Television News of the Civil Rights Era: Film & Summaries." www2.vcdh.virginia.edu/civilrightstv/wdbj/segments/WDBJ04_25.html.

Trotman, John E. Wake Forest Library. www.google.com/url?q=https://wakespace.lib.wfu.edu/bitstream/handle/10339/60992/MS615_Trotman_John_E_access.pdf&sa=D&source=docs&ust=1738270736904229&usg=AOvVaw2RO-TlzEPg4Vih0mPTx26D.

Tucker, Beverly. *Return to Fuller Street.* February 3, 2020. Historic Lexington Foundation. www.historiclexington.org/_files/ugd/03512c_cb607f7530a64bed8273e16f9343d84a.pdf.

"Urban Renewal, 1950–1966." dsl.richmond.edu/panorama/renewal/#view=0/0/1&viz=cartogram.

Virginia Tech. "Collaboration with Southside Community Is Reimagining a Historically Black College." news.vt.edu/content/news_vt_edu/en/articles/2023/07/outreach-cece-saint-pauls-college.html.

———. "Vibrant Virginia." cece.vt.edu/content/cece_vt_edu/en/VibrantVirginia.html.

Visit Hampton, VA. "Tucker Family Cemetery." visithampton.com/attraction/tucker-family-cemetery.

Wessler, Seth Freed. "Developers Found Graves in the Virginia Woods. Authorities Then Helped Erase the Historic Black Cemetery." ProPublica, December 16, 2022. www.propublica.org/article/how-authorities-erased-historic-black-cemetery-virginia.

Wikipedia. "Antão Gonçalves." en.wikipedia.org/wiki/Ant%C3%A3o_Gon%C3%A7alves.

———. "Madragana." en.wikipedia.org/wiki/Madragana.

———. "Morris Brown College." en.wikipedia.org/w/index.php?title=Morris_Brown_College&oldid=1266147658.

———. "Thomas Day (Cabinetmaker)." en.wikipedia.org/w/index.php?title=Thomas_Day_(cabinetmaker)&oldid=1261780004.

———. "Urraca Afonso." en.wikipedia.org/wiki/Urraca_Afonso.

Willis, Samantha. "The Departed and Dismissed of Richmond." Scalawag, August 5, 2019. scalawagmagazine.org/2019/08/black-graveyards.

"Wilson and Hairston Family Papers, 1751–1928—African American Documentary Resources." October 12, 2009. web.lib.unc.edu/afam/index.php/wilson-and-hairston-family-papers-1751-1928/index.html.

INDEX

ABOUT THE AUTHOR

Jeff is a writer specializing in Black history, race relations, and African diaspora studies. He received a bachelor of arts in English from Virginia Military Institute and a master of business administration from Texas A&M University–Commerce. His articles have appeared in the *Washington Post*, *Baltimore Sun*, *Virginian-Pilot*, *Cardinal News*, and *Danville Register & Bee.* Jeff can be reached at jeffbwrites@gmail.com and on Bluesky @jeffbwrites.bsky.social.